The Homesteading Recipe Book

Patricia Crawford

Collier Books
A Division of Macmillan Publishing Co., Inc.
NEW YORK

Macmillan Publishing Co., Inc.
866 Third Avenue, New York, N.Y. 10022
Collier Macmillan Canada, Ltd.

Library of Congress Cataloging in Publication Data

Crawford, Patricia, 1933–
    The homesteading recipe book.

    Includes index.
    1. Cookery (Fruit) 2. Cookery (Vegetables)
3. Fruit—Preservation. 4. Vegetables—Preservation.
I. Title.
TX811.C7   641.6′4   75-42118
ISBN 0-02-009400-0

FIRST COLLIER BOOKS EDITION 1976

The Homesteading Recipe Book is also published in a
hardcover edition by Macmillan Publishing Co., Inc.

Printed in the United States of America

Contents

Introduction

THIS small, personal recipe collection will be most useful to the new homesteader or country dweller who
may be overwhelmed by the productivity of the garden,
orchard and hen house. However, roadside stand enthusiasts
and thrifty city shoppers will find equally useful the recipes
for dealing with large quantities of fruits and vegetables
bought fresh at the height of the growing season, when prices
are lowest.

You will need larger pots, pans and bowls than you perhaps
now have if you are planning to eat your garden's produce
from spring to fall and to prepare it for winter storage: several
heavy, large (12-inch) iron skillets; large (8-, 10-, or 12-quart)
pots for cooking and sterilizing jars; large baking pans, bowls
and dishes.

If you have a choice in the matter, get a six-burner restau-
rant stove with a double oven, large grill and broiler. With
such a stove you can cook simultaneously large pots of
spaghetti gravy, vegetable soup and stewing chicken while

the three front burners are free to use for coffee or the meal at hand. Get as large a refrigerator as you can accommodate.

Pantry shelves, cold cellars, the freezer and even the garden itself are the storage areas for your kitchen. In fall stock up on flour, rice, tinned goods and all the staples that you must buy. A well-stocked pantry saves many a trip to the store which now, with the increased cost of gasoline, means saving money as well as time.

I eat country style; that is, I eat mostly what I have the most of. In spring lettuce and eggs are plentiful, so I eat salads and omelettes. In summer the table is supplied mostly from the garden. In winter I rely on my own canned and frozen fruits and vegetables, dried beans, rice and eggs. I find that eating according to the season restores anticipation to the appetite. The spring salads, the appearance of the first asparagus, are doubly enjoyable because their season is brief and I will not have them until spring comes again. A need for frugality developed this regimen; I now find I prefer it.

As food costs soar and shortages threaten, a productive garden and full pantry gain in appeal. My recipes are simple, the ingredients easily obtained. With the garden, pantry and hen house I find I can eat well, feed my guests and even make gifts of food while keeping my grocery bills down. You can do the same.

CHAPTER 1

Spring Salads and Vegetables

F R O M late February to mid-April in most of the United States, spring salads are free for the picking. Young dandelion leaves, watercress, purslane, mustard, chickweed, and sheep sorrel make delicious vitamin- and mineral-laden salads.

Look for your first salad plants in late February. Lush dandelion, purslane and sorrel are often flourishing then in sheltered spots around the house and barn, and especially in the gardens where they benefit from the extra-rich soil. Cutting these plants through early spring prevents them from flowering and spreading their seeds too thickly, so spring salad gathering is also preventive weeding.

In March and April chickweed and mustard leaves are ready to pick. These plants are good in mixed green salads but chickweed alone is too bland for most people's taste; mustard is too strongly flavored. Mix them both with cress or dandelion or use them to make store-bought lettuce go further.

1

If you are fortunate enough to have access to shady woods or cooler upland areas, you may be able to extend your wild salad season to early May. In other areas, the first hot days of spring will render most of the dandelions, sorrel and mustard too bitter for fresh use. They will be fit subjects for cooked greens.

Lettuce plants, especially loose-leafed varieties sometimes called "garden lettuce," if started indoors on March 1 and set out in a sheltered, sunny spot April 1, will be yielding leaves for the salad bowl by May 1. Sow seeds of Boston lettuce, romaine (*cos*) and iceberg a little later and set the young plants out in garden rows about April 15. Here in South Jersey garden lettuce usually remains sweet and tender until early July. Thereafter the hot summer sun soon makes it bitter. I find I can prolong the lettuce season by covering a small part of the bed with lath and burlap and keeping it well watered. Lettuce thus grown tends to be over-lush and not so tasty as that grown in open rows, but even so it is superior in quality to most of that found in the supermarket.

By the time the lettuce supply is dwindling, small summer cabbages are ready to cut for slaw and other salads. By mid-July the profusion of fresh salad ingredients from the garden—tomatoes, peppers, cucumbers, spinach, carrots, beets—make it easy to get along without lettuce.

Sow lettuce seeds for a fall supply on August 1. I prefer to sow them indoors, since they are more easily and economically kept watered and weeded on my window sill than in the garden. Three- to five-inch-tall plants are a good deal easier to see and keep weeded than are tiny seedlings. You can have garden lettuce from mid-September until the first frost. A lath and burlap frame will protect lettuce from frost and will extend the season to the first hard freeze or "black frost."

Thus, with a small garden and an assist from nature, you can easily satisfy your salad needs for nine months of the year.

If you have a greenhouse, or can construct a plastic-covered lean-to on the south side of house, garage or barn, you may be able to have homegrown lettuce through the winter months.

You can have a variety of salad vegetables from late spring to fall from a small, closely planted garden. Try to put this garden as close to the kitchen door as possible so that it is never too much trouble to pick a few cucumbers or pull radishes and scallions a few minutes before dinner. Grow parsley, basil, marjoram, summer savory and dill in this small garden so that they too are always handy.

Put a small table on the edge of your garden or outside the kitchen door so that you can cut off carrot tops, radish leaves and so on. These trimmings need never come into the house but go directly to the compost heap, which saves dirt and clutter in the kitchen. Later the table will be useful for shelling peas and beans and husking corn—jobs that should never be done in the house.

Shake herbs briskly when you pick them. Most are low growing and have dirt on the underside of their leaves. Many soil particles will fall off at a tap or shake, making the herbs easier to wash.

WILD GREENS

"FIELD SALAD"

Wash leaves of dandelion, purslane, sorrel, etc. carefully, discarding any tough or discolored outer leaves. Put the clean greens in a muslin bag (25-pound rice bags are excellent) and go outside to swing the bag in a circular windmill motion to remove most of the water. Two loosely held handfuls of young and tender greens provide one serving. Heap the greens in a large bowl and dress them with this simple garlic dressing. This recipe will dress 8 handfuls—4 servings.

DRESSING

2 cloves garlic
1/4 tsp. salt
1/4 tsp. freshly ground black pepper
5 tbsp. salad oil
2 tbsp. cider or herb vinegar

In the bottom of a bowl large enough to allow thorough tossing, smash the garlic with the salt and pepper until a paste results. Stir in the oil slowly and thoroughly, then add the vinegar. The flavor is improved if you can make this dressing about an hour ahead of time. When ready to eat, toss the greens lightly and completely so that all the dressing is taken up. You may want more salt. I prefer a good deal less salt on wild greens than on garden-grown lettuce.

DANDELION SALAD, PENNSYLVANIA STYLE

8 handfuls greens
4 slices bacon, diced fine
2 eggs
1/4 cup sugar (scant)
1/4 cup water
1/8 cup vinegar
2 hardboiled eggs, diced

Cut the greens into 1/2-inch pieces. Fry the diced bacon; do not pour off fat. Remove bacon bits with a perforated spoon and add them to the greens. Beat the eggs, sugar, water and vinegar together. Add this mixture to the bacon fat and cook over low heat until the sauce thickens. Pour the sauce over the greens; toss and garnish with diced hardboiled egg. If the

bacon does not supply sufficient saltiness, add a good pinch
of salt (1/4 tsp.) to the sauce while it is cooking.

MUSTARD SAUCE FOR GREEN SALADS

4 *tbsp. sugar*
2 *tsp. dry mustard*
1 *tsp. salt*
4 *tbsp. water*
2 *tbsp. vinegar*
2 *eggs, lightly beaten*

Combine the sugar, dry mustard and salt and mix well, making sure that all lumps of mustard are worked out. Combine
water, vinegar and eggs in a small saucepan; add dry ingredients and simmer until thick. Toss the sauce well with the
greens.

COOKED GREENS

Wild salad plants, when a little past their prime, make good
cooked greens. Wash the leaves and boil them until they are
just tender. You can serve them dressed simply with butter,
salt and pepper, or simmer them for a longer time in water
with a ham bone or salt pork.

Better yet, drain the greens and toss them with olive oil,
salt and garlic, and a good dash of lemon juice or vinegar.

Greens can also be a good accompaniment to fried rice.
Combine and simmer until thick:

1 *cup water*
1 *tbsp. cornstarch or arrowroot*
1 *tsp. sugar*
soy sauce to taste

Toss the cooked, drained greens in the sauce and serve at once.

Spinach, escarole, chinese cabbage, collards and mustard greens are all very good with these dressings.

Lettuce from the garden is best dressed very simply—salt, pepper, oil and vinegar. If you want to vary the dressing, add herbs in differing proportions and use herb-flavored vinegars. Sometimes I add a drop or two of Worcestershire sauce to the dressing. If you subtly change the dressing from day to day, you will find that family and guests will never tire of simple green salad. Only a fellow cook will realize what you are doing.

The addition of garnishes such as croutons, diced hard-boiled egg, or shavings of red cabbage or red onion will dress up a plain green salad, but don't use all of them at once or you will weaken the appeal of future variations in flavor and appearance.

French Dressing alone is good on lettuce. Use this dressing too as a base for Caper Salad Dressing and for a raw vegetable marinade (p. 11).

FRENCH DRESSING

1/2 cup vinegar
3/4 tsp. salt
1/4 tsp. pepper
1-1/2 cups olive oil

Mix vinegar, salt and pepper well, making sure that salt dissolves. Add the oil gradually, beating until thick.
Yield: 2 cups.

CAPER SALAD DRESSING

1 cup French Dressing (see previous recipe)
2 tbsp. capers, mashed
2 anchovies pounded to a paste or about 1 tbsp. tuna fish, pounded fine

1 clove garlic, grated or pressed
few drops tabasco sauce
2 hardboiled eggs, finely chopped

Combine all ingredients except eggs and mix very well so
that capers, fish and garlic are thoroughly incorporated. Toss
with the lettuce—preferably Bibb or Boston types—and garnish
with the chopped eggs.
Yield: 1 cup.

GARLIC DRESSING

1 tbsp. garlic powder
1 tsp. sugar
1 tsp. salt
1 tsp. Accent (MSG)
1 tsp. dry mustard
1/4 tsp. black pepper
1 cup salad oil
1/2 cup vinegar
1 tbsp. Worcestershire sauce
1 clove garlic, minced

Mix all dry ingredients before blending in the liquids and
fresh garlic. This keeps well in the refrigerator for about a
week.
Yield: 1-1/2 cups.

SOUR CREAM DRESSING FOR LETTUCE

1/2 tsp. sugar
1/4 tsp. salt, more or less
3 tbsp. lemon or pineapple juice (approximate)
1/2 cup sour cream

Dissolve the sugar and salt in the juice, then blend the mixture into the sour cream until the dressing is thinned but not
watery.
Yield: 1/2 cup.

COLE SLAW

1 *small head* or 1/2 *large head cabbage*
1 *small onion, diced*
2 *tbsp. diced green or red sweet pepper*
1/2 *tsp. celery seed*
boiled dressing (below)

Slice the cabbage as thinly as you can. Toss with the onion, pepper and celery seed. Add the boiled dressing and toss well. Early summer cabbage will begin to ooze water almost at once. If you like crisp slaw, make it just before dinner. If you prefer it limp, make it an hour or so ahead of time and let it chill in the refrigerator.

POTATO SALAD

4 *medium potatoes*
1 *medium onion, diced*
2 *stalks celery, diced*
double recipe of boiled dressing (below)
3 *hardboiled eggs, sliced or quartered*

Boil the potatoes in their skins until a fork goes easily to the centers. Peel at once, holding the hot potatoes on the tines of a fork. Dice and mix at once with the boiled dressing so the still warm potatoes will take up the flavor instead of merely being coated with the dressing. When the potatoes have cooled, add onion and celery, and taste for saltiness. Garnish with sliced or quartered hardboiled eggs.

BOILED DRESSING FOR COLE SLAW AND POTATO SALAD

2 *tbsp. sugar*
1 *tsp. salt*
1/2 *tsp. dry mustard*
1 *egg, lightly beaten*

2 *tbsp. water*
1 *tbsp. vinegar*

Blend dry ingredients well. Mix them with egg, water and vinegar in a small saucepan and simmer until thick. This recipe will dress a bowl of cole slaw or potato salad for 4 and can be stretched with mayonnaise if it isn't quite enough.

SABROSA SALAD

By mid-May the salad garden will supply the main ingredients for this salad. Later in the season substitute tomatoes and peppers for radishes and scallions.

2 *medium cucumbers*
12 *radishes*
6 *scallions*
1 *dill pickle*
1/4 *cup salad oil*
2 *tbsp. chopped parsley*
2 *tbsp. lemon juice*
1 *clove garlic, minced*
salt and pepper to taste

Cut cucumbers, radishes, scallions and pickle into less than bite-size chunks. Salt and pepper lightly. Toss well with the oil and parsley. Mix the lemon juice and garlic and sprinkle over the salad. This looks nice heaped on lettuce leaves but is more easily eaten when served plain in a salad bowl and accompanied by a soup spoon.

MARINADES FOR VEGETABLES

I like raw vegetables and slightly cooked fresh vegetables marinated and served cold. They are easy to prepare, attractive and colorful. They are popular with my guests and I find that luncheon leftovers disappear from the refrigerator by dinnertime.

VINAIGRETTE I (for steamed asparagus, leeks and cauliflower, raw tomatoes, onions, peppers and carrots)

1 cup French Dressing (p. 6)
1 tsp. green olives, chopped fine
1 tsp. capers, mashed
1 tsp. sweet gherkins, chopped fine
1 tsp. chives, chopped fine
1 tsp. parsley, chopped fine

Combine all ingredients well and pour over vegetables. Let stand 1/2 hour at room temperature before serving. I vary this marinade by substituting for the parsley and chives one or more of the following herbs: summer savory, thyme, dill, coriander *leaves* and lemon balm.

Yield: 1-1/4 cups.

VINAIGRETTE II (for asparagus and leeks)

1 tbsp. vinegar
1 tsp. parsley
1 tsp. tarragon
1 tsp. chives
dash each of salt, pepper and dry mustard
4 tbsp. olive oil

Mix all the ingredients thoroughly and pour over hot steamed asparagus or leeks arranged in a shallow, flat-bottomed serving dish. Let stand at room temperature at least 1 hour before serving.

MARINADE ADRIENNE

1 tsp. sugar
1 tsp. paprika

1/2 tsp. salt
1/2 tsp. dry mustard
1/2 tsp. celery seed
1/2 tsp. peppercorns (about 8)
1/2 cup wine vinegar
3/4 cup salad oil

Combine sugar, paprika, salt and mustard, mixing thoroughly to remove any mustard lumps. Pound celery seeds and peppercorns in a mortar. Mix all the spices in the vinegar until sugar and salt are dissolved. Gradually stir in the oil.

Yield: 1-1/4 cups—enough to marinate 3 lbs. vegetables.

VEGETABLE MARINADE
(for carrots, turnips and potatoes)

1 lb. raw vegetables—carrots, turnips or potatoes
2 cloves garlic
1 tbsp. chopped onion
3 tbsp. salad oil
1/4 cup vinegar
1 tsp. salt
1/2 tsp. dry mustard
1 tbsp. pickling spices
1 onion, sliced and separated into rings

Cut the root vegetables into julienne strips.

Sauté the garlic and chopped onion in the oil until tender. Stir in the vinegar. Mix the salt and mustard together and add to the mixture. Tie the pickling spices in a piece of cheesecloth and add along with the vegetable strips. Simmer about 5 minutes—the vegetables should be quite firm. Remove the bag of pickling spices and put the mixture into a flat-bottomed dish. Refrigerate for at least 4 hours—overnight is better. Drain just before serving and garnish with the onion rings. Serves 4.

AGLIO-OLIO

This is the fondue of the salad season. Dip the vegetables in the sauce and eat. A variety of fresh vegetables, a bowl of aglio-olio and a loaf of good bread make a good summer lunch. Don't use a tablecloth when you serve aglio-olio.

> 6 cloves garlic
> 4 egg yolks
> 1/2 tsp. salt
> 2 cups olive oil (salad oil will do) at room temperature
> juice of 1 lemon

Mash the garlic in the bottom of a bowl; stir in the egg yolks and salt. Stir in very gradually 3 tbsp. oil. Stir in the lemon juice. Now blend in the remaining oil, a little at a time, until the sauce is thick.

Put the bowl in the center of the table and surround it with cooked new redskin potatoes, carrot strips, artichokes, beet slices, cauliflower florets, hardboiled eggs, steamed and chilled asparagus spears, etc.

Aglio-olio is a fine dressing for most salads and fish.

RED CABBAGE IN MARINADE

Begin this dish 4 days ahead of time.

> 1 head red cabbage (2-3 lbs.)
> salt
> 10 peppercorns, crushed
> 1 bay leaf
> 1 clove garlic, pressed
> 2 cups vinegar

Remove the core and thick ribs of the cabbage. Shred cabbage and arrange in layers in a flat-bottomed bowl, sprinkling each layer lightly with salt. Let stand for 48 hours, turning occasionally. Drain. Put the cabbage in a bowl with the pepper, bay leaf and garlic. Cover with hot (near boiling) vinegar. Let marinate for 48 hours. Drain and serve. Serves 4.

SWEET AND SOUR CABBAGE

olive oil to cover bottom of large skillet
2 medium onions, sliced thin
1 small cabbage (about 2 lbs.), shredded, cored and ribs
   removed
3 tomatoes, peeled and seeded
2 tbsp. wine vinegar
salt and pepper to taste
1 tbsp. sugar

Heat a large skillet, and put in the oil and onions. Sauté until onions are limp. Stir in the cabbage, tomatoes, vinegar, salt and pepper. Simmer about 10 minutes. Stir in the sugar. Stir-toss a minute or two and serve. Serves 4.

CUCUMBERS

A half dozen plants will provide cucumbers for the table from mid-May to mid-July. Use the almost daily harvest in a variety of ways—as salad, cooked vegetable, fresh relish and entrée. Pick cucumbers when they are young, slim and firm. The first ones of the season can simply be peeled and cut into slim spears. Chill them and serve sprinkled with salt and lemon juice.

An easily and quickly prepared salad is thinly sliced young cucumbers, sprinkled lightly with salt and vinegar and garnished with paper-thin raw onion rings. Sprinkle the dish with cracked ice and serve at once.

A marvelous cooling cucumber salad for hot days, and a perfect accompaniment for curried dishes at any season, is chopped cucumber dressed with yogurt and lemon juice. A half cup of plain yogurt and 1 tbsp. lemon juice will dress 2 medium-sized chopped cucumbers. To make a sauce for curry, double the amount of yogurt. Vary this dish by the addition of one small onion, finely chopped, or by occasionally garnishing with finely chopped fresh mint leaves. From time to time substitute sour cream for yogurt.

FRESH CUCUMBER SALAD

This is good served in a small cup of lettuce leaves and is an equally fine relish to accompany roast pork or meat loaf.

> 1 cucumber (5 or 6 inches), chopped fine
> 2 scallions, chopped fine
> 4 radishes, chopped fine
> 1/2 tsp. dried thyme or 1 tsp. fresh thyme leaves
> 1/4 cup vinegar
> 2 tbsp. sugar
> salt to taste

Mix all ingredients and let chill, stirring occasionally, for at least 2 hours before serving. Taste after one hour. If the vinegar taste is too strong, add a small amount of water to the relish.

FRIED CUCUMBER ROUNDS

> 2 medium cucumbers
> garlic salt
> 1/4 cup flour
> 1/4 cup breadcrumbs
> oil
> parmesan or romano cheese, grated

Slice unpeeled cucumbers in 1/4-inch-thick rounds and sprinkle with garlic salt. Coat the rounds with a mixture of the flour and breadcrumbs. Fry lightly in the oil. After you turn the rounds over, sprinkle the fried side with cheese. When both sides are done, transfer the rounds to a heated serving plate. Young zucchini squash is also very good prepared this way. Serves 4.

TUNA STUFFED CUCUMBERS

This is a good quick entrée for a summer lunch—especially if you have leftover rice on hand.

> 2 *five-inch cucumbers*
> 1 *can (6-1/2 oz.) tuna fish*
> 1/2 *cup cold cooked rice*
> 4 *tbsp. mayonnaise*
> 2 *tbsp. minced onion*
> 1/2 *tsp. salt*
> 1 *tbsp. lemon juice*

Cut the unpeeled cucumbers in half lengthwise and scoop out the pulp. Combine the remaining ingredients and pack the stuffing well into the cucumbers, mounding them smoothly. Chill well and serve. Serves 4.

BAKED STUFFED CUCUMBERS

This dish is different, attractive to serve and economical.

4 five-inch cucumbers
4 tbsp. butter
2 tbsp. onion, chopped
1/2 cup breadcrumbs
1 cup cooked pork, veal or chicken, minced
1 tbsp. toasted sesame seeds, pounded in mortar
1/2 tsp. salt
1/2 tsp. dried thyme leaves or oregano
1/2 cup water
2 tsp. soy sauce

Slice 1/2 inch from each cucumber lengthwise and scoop out the pulp. Melt the butter and sauté the onion. Add the breadcrumbs, meat, sesame seeds, salt and thyme. Mix the water and soy sauce and add to the mixture to moisten it, blending thoroughly. Stuff the cucumber boats and arrange them in a baking pan, using crinkled foil to keep them right side up. Put about 1/2 inch of water in the pan. Bake at 350° for 30 minutes or until the cucumber shells are tender. Serves 4.

Radishes are best served ice cold with a salt cellar as their only accompaniment. For variety's sake try this Japanese radish relish, which goes well with broiled fish and rice dishes.

1/2 tbsp. sugar
2 tbsp. soy sauce
1 tbsp. vinegar
15 radishes, sliced thin

Dissolve the sugar in the soy sauce and vinegar. Pour over the radishes and mix.

Zucchini is often mistreated and overcooked until it disintegrates into an unappetizing soup-like consistency. Barely cooked zucchini is more attractive and tastes much better. Pick zucchini when they are less than half their size at maturity—about 10 inches long—shiny and firm, and when the seeds inside have just begun to form. Cut off the stem and blossom ends of the squash. Do not peel. Cut the zucchini into generous bite-size pieces and boil in as little water as possible until the chunks are barely tender—about 3 minutes for young zucchini. Quickly drain off the water and add about 3 tbsp. butter to the pan; sprinkle well with garlic salt and shake the pan until the butter is melted and the zucchini well coated. Serve at once.

RHUBARB

Rhubarb is a hardy perennial spring vegetable that we use mostly like a fruit. Two or three clumps of rhubarb will supply a family of four in late spring and early summer, with enough left over for a few jars of rhubarb jam and chutney. Plant rhubarb roots in spring or fall in a deeply dug bed into which has been incorporated plenty of compost, rotted manure and wood ash. Do not pull any stalks the first year. Do not let a flowering stalk set blossoms. Stop pulling rhubarb July 1; give the bed a top dressing of fertilizer or compost and let it rest until the following spring.

Rhubarb is ready to eat when the stalks pull out easily from the center of the clump.

Rhubarb leaves contain oxalic acid and should not be eaten by man or beast. Only the stalks are edible.

The first dish of spring rhubarb may prove to be quite laxative. Della Lutes in *The Country Kitchen* writes: "The first rhubarb of the season is to the digestive tract of winter inner logged man what a good hot bath with plenty of healing soap is to the outer after a bout with plough and harrow.

Even the tongue and teeth have a scrubbed feeling after a dish of early rhubarb."

Have stewed rhubarb for breakfast, make a pie or two, put up a few jars of jam and chutney. Then forget about rhubarb until next spring. It is best eaten in its own brief season.

STEWED RHUBARB

3 *cups rhubarb*
1 *cup sugar*
1 *tsp. baking soda*
water

Cut the rhubarb into 1/2-inch pieces and put into a saucepan with just enough water to cover the bottom. Sprinkle with the sugar and baking soda. Cook gently until tender. Young rhubarb will cook in 5 to 7 minutes. Tougher, older stalks may require as long as 15 minutes.

BAKED RHUBARB

3 *cups rhubarb*
1-1/2 *cups sugar*
2 *tbsp. lemon or orange juice*

Mix rhubarb, sugar and juice. Spoon into baking dish and bake, covered, at 350° for about 30 minutes or until tender.

RHUBARB PIE

1 *cup water*
2 *cups sugar*
1 *tsp. baking soda*
5 *cups rhubarb*
5 *tbsp. cornstarch*

9-inch pie shell, already baked and cooled
whipped cream or sour cream

Boil water and sugar together; add baking soda and rhubarb. Lower heat and cook gently until the rhubarb is tender. Pour off the syrup and heat. Make a solution of the cornstarch and a little water and stir into the hot syrup. As soon as the syrup thickens and clears, add the rhubarb. Remove from heat and let the mixture cool to lukewarm. Pour into the pie shell and chill. Top with whipped cream or sour cream before serving.

As the rhubarb season ends, strawberries begin to come in. A delightful combination is Strawberry-Rhubarb Pie. Simply substitute 2 cups hulled, halved strawberries for 2 cups of rhubarb.

RHUBARB JAM

This recipe is from Berks County, Pennsylvania. It takes a little longer than more modern recipes but makes a superior jam.

15 cups rhubarb (5 lbs.)
5 lbs. sugar
1-inch piece fresh ginger root, bruised
grated rind and juice of 2 lemons

Cut the rhubarb into 1-inch pieces and put into a stoneware crock or an enamel or stainless steel kettle. Cover with the sugar and let stand 2 days. Strain off and boil the juice. Pour the hot juice over the rhubarb and let stand one day. Add the ginger root, lemon rind and juice, and boil jam until it thickens. Ladle into hot, sterilized jars and seal.

Yield: About 6 pints.

RHUBARB CHUTNEY

4 cups rhubarb, sliced in 1/2-inch pieces
pulp of 1 orange
1 clove garlic, crushed
1/2 lb. brown sugar
1 cup vinegar
1 lb. raisins
1 tsp. chili pepper, ground

Combine all ingredients and stir over low heat until sugar is dissolved. Bring to a gentle boil and stir frequently until the chutney thickens. Ladle into hot jars and seal.

Yield: 1-1/2 pints.

ASPARAGUS

Try to find space in your garden for an asparagus bed. Asparagus is perennial so put it to one side of the garden, along with the rhubarb, where it will not be injured by the annual tilling. Plant 8 one-year-old roots for each mouth you want to feed. Do not cut any stalks the first year. Set good quality roots 18 inches apart in rows 3 feet apart. Keep the bed weeded, watered and well fertilized and you will have asparagus every spring for the next 15 years. Cut the spears about 1 inch below the surface of the ground with a sharp knife or regular asparagus knife, being careful not to injure the roots.

If you buy asparagus from a roadside stand, buy a crate at a time. A crate, which is twelve bunches, weighs between 24 and 30 pounds. This is a lot of asparagus. However, in two hours you can freeze enough to last well into winter and prepare the rest to refrigerate for immediate use. Two bunches of asparagus will provide generous helpings for a family of four at four meals. Divide two bunches into four piles and snap off the tough white ends; wash, drain and store the spears in plastic bags in the refrigerator, where they will stay crisp for a week to 10 days.

The remaining ten bunches in the crate will yield 16 to 18 pints of frozen asparagus whose value will appreciate considerably as prices rise in autumn.

To freeze asparagus snap off the white ends, wash the spears, and sort into thin, medium and thick sizes. Cut the spears to the height of your freezer containers or into 1-inch pieces. Heat the asparagus in boiling water: thin spears, 2 minutes; medium, 3 minutes; thick, 5 minutes. Cool the spears at once in cold water and drain. Pack the spears in freezer containers, leaving no head space; seal and freeze immediately.

The first asparagus of the season is best served steamed— 6 or 7 minutes at the most—so that it is barely tender, still crisp and firm. Put the spears in a colander if you don't have a steamer. Put the colander in a kettle over an inch or so of boiling water. Cover it tightly and steam until just tender. Remove at once and arrange spears on a heated serving dish. Salt them lightly and serve with butter.

ASPARAGUS VINAIGRETTE

This can double as a vegetable or a hot weather salad.

24 spears asparagus, steamed
1 tbsp. wine vinegar
1 tsp. parsley, chopped very fine
1 tsp. tarragon, chopped very fine
1 tsp. chives, chopped
1/4 tsp. dry mustard
1/4 tsp. salt
4 tbsp. olive oil

Arrange asparagus in a flat-bottomed serving dish. Combine remaining ingredients and pour over asparagus. Let stand at room temperature 1 hour, turning spears occasionally so they marinate evenly. Serves 4.

SAUTERNE BAKED ASPARAGUS

24 spears asparagus, steamed
salt and pepper
4 tbsp. melted butter
1/4 cup sauterne
3 tbsp. Parmesan cheese, grated

Arrange the asparagus in a baking dish. Salt and pepper lightly; sprinkle with butter, wine and cheese. Bake at 400° for 10 minutes. Serves 4.

AMBUSHED ASPARAGUS

This recipe is alleged to have survived since colonial days. It's fine for a Lenten or vegetarian lunch, a New Year's Day brunch or any fancy breakfast.

4 hard rolls
melted butter
1 cup white sauce, made with cream
1 cup asparagus, steamed and cut into less than bite-size bits
1/4 tsp. nutmeg
1/4 tsp. paprika

Cut the tops off the rolls and scoop out centers. Brush the inside of the rolls with the melted butter and put rolls and tops in 250° oven for a few minutes to crisp.

Heat the cream sauce and stir in the asparagus, nutmeg and paprika. Remove the rolls from the oven and reset oven at 350°. Spoon the mixture into the rolls, cap with the tops and return them to the oven for 5 minutes. If rolls tend to fall over, use crinkled foil to keep them upright in the baking pan. Serves 4.

ASPARAGUS PURÉE

If you have asparagus stalks left over after trimming for the freezer or from a recipe calling for tips only, purée the leftovers.

> *asparagus*
> *1 slice onion to each 1/2 cup asparagus*
> *1/2 cup water for each cup asparagus*

Cook asparagus and onion in water until tender. Purée in blender. Freeze at once or use in a day or two for soup.

CREAM OF ASPARAGUS SOUP

> *2 tbsp. butter*
> *2 tbsp. flour*
> *2 cups asparagus purée*
> *1 cup water*
> *1 cup light cream*
> *salt and pepper to taste*

Melt butter and blend in flour. Slowly add and blend in puréed asparagus. Add the water and cream. Salt and pepper to taste. Heat to just short of scalding and serve. In winter thicken this soup with a few tablespoons of puréed mashed potatoes for extra heartiness.

CHAPTER 2

Summer: Season of Surplus

By July 4 home gardens, farmers' markets and roadside stands provide a variety and abundance of freshly picked, top quality vegetables and fruit. Tomatoes, peppers and eggplant seem always to produce more than the home gardener expects or knows what to do with. All three are so versatile that the vegetable recipes in this chapter will concentrate on them. By using the big three in a variety of ways during the season, you can avoid waste and achieve a real reduction in the grocery budget. Canning and preserving the surplus will extend the garden-based economy throughout the entire year.

TOMATOES

The date of the introduction of the tomato into western Europe and its provenience is a matter of some dispute.

Elizabeth David in *Italian Food* writes that in the late Middle Ages pasta began to be eaten with tomatoes, "the cultivation of which dated from the time when one Fra Serenio brought the precious seeds on his return from China." A more commonly held belief is that the Spanish conquistadors brought the tomato to Europe in the 16th century. Arthur J. Simons in the *New Vegetable Grower's Handbook* states that the physician Galen knew all about the tomato in 200 A.D. while *The Cooking of Italy* (Time-Life Books, 1968) flatly declares that "no European had ever set eyes on it [the tomato] before Cortes conquered Mexico."

Whatever its origin, the versatile tomato has become a staple. Serve it for breakfast, lunch, dinner and dessert. Additional recipes in Chapter 5 will provide more ways to preserve tomatoes in relishes, ketchup, jam, pickles and marmalade.

If you buy tomatoes by the bushel at a farmers' market or roadside stand, you will find they are a good deal cheaper than by the pound at the supermarket. Even more economical are "off-the-grader" tomatoes. Ask for these at roadside stands, if you will be able to deal with the tomatoes directly you arrive home. "Off-the-grader" tomatoes will usually be dead ripe, some with soft spots or misshapen. There will be some waste but they are still an excellent buy for the home canner and relish maker.

One bushel of tomatoes will weigh about 53 pounds (about 160 medium-size tomatoes) and will yield 15 to 20 quarts of canned tomatoes. When you get them home, pick out the ripest, most perfect ones and refrigerate them for slicing and salads. Put the unripe or partially ripe out of direct sunlight for a few days to ripen and redden. Select the best-looking for stuffing.

TOMATOES FOR BREAKFAST

FRIED TOMATOES

I fry a platterful of these tomatoes for Sunday morning breakfast and keep them warm in the oven while I fix eggs and sausage. They're a good summer substitute for fried potatoes in the morning. Any meaty tomato can be fried but if you grow or can buy large yellow tomatoes (preferably Burpee's Golden Jubilee), you'll find them best.

8 *medium-size tomatoes*
1 *cup flour*
1 *tsp. salt*
1 *tbsp. sugar*
4 *tbsp. bacon drippings*

Core tomatoes and slice about 1/2-inch thick. Slice off and discard the rounded blossom ends—they never fry nicely. Mix the flour, salt and sugar in a small bowl. Heat a large skillet and, when it is hot, add 2 tbsp. of the bacon drippings. Coat the tomato slices with the flour mixture and fry on both sides. Transfer the fried slices to a platter and keep warm in oven until all are done and the rest of the meal is ready. You will need the additional drippings for successive panfuls.

TOMATO SAUSAGE

Use a dozen of these at once and freeze the rest for a late fall breakfast surprise.

2 *cups cooked rice*
2 *cups breadcrumbs*
2 *cups tomato purée (see p. 33)*
2 *tbsp. onion, finely chopped*
2 *tsp. thyme or sage, crumbled*

1 *tsp. fresh basil, chopped fine*
salt to taste
3 *oz. small pork sausage casings*

Mix the first 7 ingredients and stuff lightly into the sausage casings. Twist casing and tie every 3 inches to form links. Sauté in bacon fat until cooked through and evenly brown on all sides.

SANDWICHES

Bacon, lettuce and tomato sandwiches, the standard BLTs we all know so well, take on new life when fresh, ripe tomatoes can be used generously and the lettuce, too, is straight from the garden. Salt the tomato slices and sprinkle them with fresh or dried oregano. From time to time add a thin layer of bread-and-butter pickles to the interior of a BLT, or very thin slices of dill pickles (p. 146).

A grilled tomato and cheese sandwich is greatly enlivened by sprinkling the tomato slices with salt, freshly ground black pepper and crumbled oregano. For a subtle taste change, sprinkle the slices with vinegar. Chop and add to the sandwich filling any leftover bits of pepperoni, salami or breakfast bacon.

Open-face broiled tomato and cheese sandwiches on a platter, a bowl of potato salad and a colorful relish tray make a complete, light and easy-to-fix lunch.

Arrange buttered slices of homemade, French or Italian bread on a baking sheet and broil until lightly toasted. Turn the slices over and put a layer of American or provolone (mild) cheese on each. Slide back under broiler for a few minutes until cheese begins to bubble. Do not let yourself be distracted for even a moment at this point, or the cheese is sure to burn. Remove from broiler, apply salted tomato slices and return to broiler for another 3 or 4 minutes. Dust with fresh ground black pepper and oregano.

SALADS

The plainest tomato salad, of course, consists of sliced tomatoes on a bed of lettuce. Vary this instant standby with mayonnaise spiced with crushed capers or very fine diced dill pickle. Or sprinkle the tomatoes with vinaigrette or French dressing.

SALAD NIÇOISE

This salad is rich, filling and attractive. A bowl of Niçoise, an omelette and a basket of hot rolls make a fine summer lunch or light supper.

> 2 2-oz. *tins anchovy fillets*
> 2 *cloves garlic, pressed*
> 1/4 *cup olive oil*
> 2 *tbsp. wine vinegar*
> 5 *sprigs parsley, chopped*
> 2 *green peppers*
> 6 *medium tomatoes*
> 6 *scallions*
> 12 *ripe olives, pitted*

Drain the oil from the anchovies into the bottom of the salad bowl. Add garlic, olive oil, vinegar and chopped parsley. Blend well. Seed the peppers and cut into thin strips. Cut the tomatoes into 5 or 6 pieces each. Chop the scallions, including some of the green tops. Cut the olives in half. Combine all ingredients in the salad bowl and toss well with the dressing. Do not salt before you taste, as the anchovies and their oil usually provide sufficient saltiness. Let the salad chill at least one hour before serving.

This is one salad that provides good leftovers. If there is only a little Niçoise left, use it to dress up steak sandwiches.

TOMATO-TUNA SALAD

5 tbsp. olive oil
2 tbsp. wine vinegar
1 tsp. salt
1 tsp. fresh rosemary leaves or 1/2 tsp. dry leaves, crumbled
1 3-1/2-oz. can tuna fish
5 medium tomatoes

Mix together the oil, vinegar, salt, rosemary and tuna in a bowl. Coarsely chop the tomatoes and mix well with the dressing. The tuna fish here is a condiment. Flake it and disperse it so well through the salad that its presence is not immediately obvious. Serve on a lettuce bed and accompany with lemon wedges.

TOMATOES STUFFED WITH CHICKEN SALAD

Select medium-sized, ripe, well-shaped tomatoes. Cut off stem end and scoop out seeds. Turn tomatoes upside down to drain for about 10 minutes before stuffing. Sprinkle the inside of tomato shells with salt and lemon juice. Stuff with chicken salad. One tomato nicely stuffed and domed will hold about 1/2 cup salad.

TOMATOES AS A COOKED VEGETABLE

STEWED TOMATOES

Good by themselves, stewed tomatoes go especially well with codfish cakes. Some people like to mix them with mashed potatoes.

6 *ripe tomatoes*
4 *tbsp. butter*
1 *tbsp. fresh basil, chopped* or 1 *tsp. dried leaves, crumbled*
1 *tbsp. brown sugar*
salt and pepper to taste
1 *tbsp. cornmeal*

Peel and seed tomatoes; dice them and put into a saucepan with the butter. Let stew about 5 minutes. Add basil, sugar, salt and pepper, and cornmeal. Cook gently, stirring frequently for 10 minutes.

BAKED TOMATOES

10 *medium tomatoes, cored, peeled and quartered*
1 *stalk celery, diced*
1 *medium onion, diced*
1 *tsp. sugar*
1 *tsp. salt*
dash tabasco sauce
1 *tsp. dried thyme*
1/2 *cup toasted, buttered breadcrumbs*

Mix all ingredients except the breadcrumbs and turn into a buttered casserole. Bake at 350° for 30 minutes. Sprinkle the breadcrumbs over the tomatoes and return to the oven for about 10 minutes or slide under the broiler until the crumbs begin to brown. To vary, mix 1/2 cup cottage cheese or chopped mozzarella into the mixture before baking. Serves 4 generously.

FRESH TOMATO SOUP

This is especially good on those occasional chilly, cloudy days of summer and early fall.

> 5 *medium tomatoes*
> 1 *onion, diced*
> 1 *tsp. salt*
> 2 *cups beef consommé*
> 1 *tsp. fresh summer savory or thyme*

Peel and seed tomatoes; put into a saucepan with onion, and cook until soft. Put the mixture into the blender to liquify or rub through a sieve. Return mixture to the pan; add salt and consommé. Heat to almost boiling. Remove from heat and stir in the savory or thyme. For extra-rich soup, substitute 1 cup cream for 1 cup consommé. Serves 4.

TOMATO GRAVY

This recipe will make enough gravy for two spaghetti dinners for a family of four, or 8 servings. If you are having pasta only once in a while, freeze half the gravy for use in lasagna or pizza.

If you are feeding children or guests who may be something less than expert at spaghetti twirling, prepare rigatoni or maruzze (shells). These forms of pasta are bite-size, easily managed with a fork and much less likely to stain white shirts and tablecloths. On the other hand, if you want to gauge the expertise of a pasta fancier, serve perciatelli, a thicker, hollow, spaghetti-like type of pasta that is difficult to manage.

1/4 cup olive or peanut oil
1 large onion, diced fine
2 cloves garlic, slivered
1/4 cup (6 good sprigs) parsley, chopped
1 tbsp. basil, chopped
1 bay leaf
20 medium tomatoes, peeled, cored and chopped or
    2 qts. canned tomatoes
salt and sugar to taste

Heat a large, heavy-bottomed saucepan. Pour in oil and add onions. When onions become transparent, remove the pan from the heat and add the garlic slivers, parsley, basil, bay leaf and tomatoes. Put on low heat and simmer about 3 hours, stirring occasionally. Sauce will thicken considerably. Add salt to taste, and a dash of sugar if the gravy is too tart. To make a thicker sauce, add a 6-oz. can of tomato paste with the canned tomatoes.

If you wish, add meatballs (p. 134) when gravy begins to thicken.

CANNING TOMATOES

Home-canned tomatoes in quantity on the pantry shelf are a reassuring sight. Put up tomatoes in quart jars for spaghetti gravy, in pints for stewing and adding to bean and vegetable soups. A dozen or so half-pint jars are handy for individual servings or for making taco and enchilada sauce.

The most tedious part of tomato canning is peeling and coring. Try to have a guest or two on hand during canning season. Seat the guest on a stool and place on the table before him (or her) a large kettle and a basin. Give him a sharp paring knife and put within his reach a box of tissues and a glass of something cold.

Scald a colander full of tomatoes at a time and put them in front of the guest. He will core them and slip off the skins. Make sure he works over the kettle so that none of the juice is lost and mess is minimized. The cores and skins go in the basin. Meanwhile you can assemble your jars, lids and rings and the canning kettle with rack for processing. When you have a nice kettleful of prepared tomatoes, put them on medium heat and bring them to a boil. Reduce the heat a little and boil them gently for 5 minutes. Ladle the tomatoes into hot jars, to 1/2 inch of the top; apply lids and rings, and process in boiling water for 10 minutes.

Use only ripe, sound tomatoes. Remove seeds if they bother you or if you are watching your weight.

TOMATO PURÉE

Core ripe, perfect tomatoes—do not peel. Slice or quarter the tomatoes and cook them over a low flame until they are quite soft. Put them through a fine sieve. Cook the sieved pulp until it thickens to purée consistency. Ladle into hot jars, seal, and process in boiling water 10 minutes.

PEPPERS

Peppers have become so expensive that if you are at all fond of them, it will pay you to grow about a dozen plants in your home garden. Pepper bushes will produce until early fall if you keep them picked. A dozen plants will supply a family of four with peppers for stuffing, salads and frying, with enough left over for some freezer packets and a few jars of relish. I find I use about a pepper a day—to chop into omelettes, eggplant stuffing, Swiss steak, scallopine, potato salad, etc. When weight watchers visit I fill a four-part relish dish with crisp pepper strips, carrot sticks and stalks of celery and fennel. This is colorful and appeals to everyone—especially on a hot summer day.

If you are especially fond of fried peppers, grow a dozen plants of a long, light green variety.

Freeze small packets of cored, blanched peppers for winter use in vegetable soup and stews. Blanch a few sprigs of parsley and some celery tops and freeze with 2 or 3 peppers in packs. This handy combination will season soups, chicken *a la cacciatori,* creamed chicken, etc. in winter when you may not have these vegetables fresh on hand.

FRIED PEPPERS

16 peppers
3 tbsp. olive oil
2 cloves garlic, crushed
salt to taste

Core and seed peppers and slice into strips. Plunge peppers into boiling water for one minute. Drain in colander and shake well, or toss in paper towels or a tea towel to dry so they will not spatter when they fry. Heat a large skillet, and put in olive oil and garlic. Let the garlic fry until it begins to brown; remove garlic and add peppers. Stir-fry over a medium flame about 5 minutes, salt to taste and serve. Serves 4.

Refrigerate any leftovers to use on steak sandwiches or simply as a cold snack next day.

PEPPERS IN CREAM

I've had this pepper dish in Mexico, where it goes well with tortillas to scoop up the sauce. It's also very good mixed with plain boiled or steamed rice.

6 *sweet green peppers*
3 *tbsp. butter*
1/2 *tsp. salt*
1 *cup cream*

Toast peppers over flame or in oven until skin wrinkles, and peel. Remove the core and seeds and cut the peppers into narrow strips. Fry the strips in butter over a low flame until tender. Mix the salt into the cream and pour over the peppers and butter. Simmer 2 or 3 minutes, stirring thoroughly. Sprinkle with paprika or nutmeg and serve. Serves 4.

STUFFED PEPPERS

This recipe evolved by accident and looks unlikely, but it has become quite popular here. It is good hot or cold. The ham and olive mixture first used was leftover sandwich filling. The addition of pickle juice was the inspiration of a then quite young guest.

4 *bell peppers, preferably of a shape to sit up by them-selves*
1-1/2 *cups ham*
1/2 *cup pitted green olives*
2 *tbsp. juice from sweet pickles or bread-and-butter pickles*

Slice off the tops and remove seeds from the peppers. Plunge them in boiling water for one minute. Let cool. Put the ham and olives through the medium blade of the food mill and mix with pickle juice. Stuff the peppers, put into a baking dish in about 1 inch of water, and bake at 350° 15 minutes.

PEPPERS AND SAUSAGE

This is a cold weather lunch entrée. Ladled into long Italian rolls, it makes a good hot sandwich.

1-1/2 lbs. sausage
4 peppers
1 cup tomato gravy (p. 31) or 1 cup tomato purée sea-
    soned with 1/2 tsp. oregano, 1/4 tsp. garlic salt and
    one bay leaf

Fry sausage lightly until browned on all sides and drain well.
Seed peppers, if fresh, and heat in boiling water. Cut peppers
in strips. Arrange sausages and peppers in baking dish and
pour over them the tomato gravy or seasoned purée. Bake at
350° for 20 minutes. Serves 4.

ROASTED PEPPERS

Serve these as a relish with meat or as part of an antipasto.
Roast peppers taste best if they have been roasted over a real
fire—tabletop hibachis and barbecue grills are fine. Otherwise,
roast them in a hot oven or under the broiler until the skin
turns brown and wrinkles, when the skin will peel off easily.

8 peppers, roasted and peeled
1 clove garlic, sliced
5 tbsp. olive oil
1 tbsp. lemon juice
1/4 tsp. salt

Seed peppers and cut in strips. Mix garlic, oil, lemon juice
and salt thoroughly until salt is dissolved. Put the pepper strips
in a deep bowl, a quart jar or a small straight-sided crock. Pour
the oil mixture over them and let them marinate at least 3
hours, stirring gently from time to time. Remove the garlic
slivers before serving.

EGGPLANT

Eggplant in this country is too little appreciated and
often mistreated. Supermarkets frequently offer only large,

dull, scarred fruits that have been left too long on the bush, so that their seeds have developed and the skin has become tough and bitter. Mature eggplant has a strong taste that many people find objectionable. If you grow your own, you can harvest eggplant at the peak of perfection—when they are about half the size they would be at maturity, shiny and firm. The seeds will be inconspicuous and the skin quite edible. If you shop for eggplant at roadside stands and find only large ones on display, ask for what you want. Most farmers will be happy to meet your requirements.

Many of us are familiar with only two ways of preparing eggplant—breaded and deep-fried, and *a la parmigiana* with cheese and a tomato sauce. Both are good. However, fried foods are not always compatible with hot weather. The following dishes are comparatively light, cool and simple to prepare.

MARINATED EGGPLANT

3 *young eggplants (about 8 inches long)*
1/3 *cup white vinegar*
2 *cloves garlic, bruised*
1 *tsp. fresh oregano leaves or 1/2 tsp. dried leaves*
1/2 *tsp. salt*
1/2 *cup olive oil or peanut oil*

Slice off the stem and blossom ends and dice eggplant into bite-size pieces. Simmer in water until tender (5 to 7 minutes). Drain the eggplant well in a colander and then toss to dry in a tea towel or pat with paper towels. Combine the vinegar, garlic, oregano and salt in a deep bowl. Add the eggplant and toss well. Let marinate for at least 1 hour. Fifteen minutes before serving, remove the garlic clove and add the oil, tossing well.

Refrigerated leftovers should be restored to room temperature before serving, since the cold oil thickens and becomes unattractively opaque. Serves 4 generously.

FRESH EGGPLANT PICKLE

2 *young eggplants (about 8 inches long)*
juice of 1 lemon
3 *sprigs parsley, very finely chopped*
1/4 *cup olive oil*
1 *clove garlic, pressed*
1/4 *tsp. salt*

Boil the whole eggplants until they soften slightly. Remove stem and blossom ends. Cube the eggplants and put the cubes in a deep bowl. Mix the lemon juice, parsley, oil, garlic and salt and pour over the eggplant. Let marinate overnight if possible. About 1/2 hour before serving, drain off the marinade, cover the bowl tightly and refrigerate. This unsubtle fresh pickle is best served very cold on a very hot day.

BAKED EGGPLANT

This delicious and different treatment of eggplant is simplicity itself to prepare, and can be baked during the last half hour or so of a meatloaf's or oven roast's baking time.

1 *medium onion*
1 *green pepper*
1 *tbsp. butter*
1/2 *tsp. turmeric*
1 *tsp. garam masala (p. 166)*
1/4 *tsp. chili powder*
1 *tsp. lemon juice*
1 *tsp. salt*
1 *medium eggplant*

Mince the onion and pepper. Heat a small frying pan and put in the butter, turmeric, garam masala and chili. Cook the spices, stirring constantly for 2 minutes so that they "cure" and acquire a mellow taste. Now add the onion, peppers, lemon juice, and salt. Cook and stir until all the liquid is taken up and the mixture is dry.

Make 2 deep parallel slits lengthwise in the eggplant and stuff the onion-pepper mixture in the slits. Wrap the eggplant in aluminum foil and bake at 350° about 30 minutes. Test the eggplant by squeezing gently, using a pot holder. When the eggplant is soft and gives under the fingers, it is done. Slice it as you would a cake, discarding the stem end. Serve the slices, skin and all. Some people will like the skin, others will leave it.

You can change the accent from Indian to Italian by using this stuffing in a medium eggplant.

1 *tomato*
2 *anchovy fillets*
1 *clove garlic, pressed*
1/4 *tsp. salt*
1 *tsp. parsley, very finely chopped*
1/4 *cup oil*

Peel, core, seed and chop the tomato into a small bowl. Dice the anchovies and add to the tomatoes along with the garlic, salt, parsley and oil. Mix well and stuff into eggplant slits.

EGGPLANT KAZAYUKI

2 *young eggplants (about 8 inches long)*
3 *tsp. salad oil*
2 *medium tomatoes*
1–2 *tbsp. soy sauce, according to taste*

Remove the ends and cut eggplants into bite-size cubes. Sauté in the hot oil, stirring so that the cubes are all slightly cooked on all sides. Remove from fire. Peel and chop the tomatoes and add to the eggplant. Stir in soy sauce to taste. Cover and simmer until eggplant is tender—about 10 minutes. Be wary

of salting this dish, since the soy sauce provides enough
saltiness for many palates.

RATATOUILLE

My version of this dish is best known around the house
as "vegetable glop" and is by far the favorite vegetable dish
of summer. Until early August the zucchini may overshadow
the eggplant. When the zucchini season ends, the eggplant is
the dominant element. This recipe fills a large shallow baking
dish and will serve four generously. You will find that most
people have a second helping and thereafter have "just one
more spoonful," so that there is scarcely any left by the end
of the meal.

> 3 *young eggplants (about 8 inches)*
>   or 3 *young zucchinis (about 8 inches)*
>   or *any combination of the two, according to what you
>   have*
> 1/2 *cup flour*
> 1/4 *tsp. salt*
> *salad oil as needed*
> 2 *medium green bell peppers, seeded and coarsely
>   chopped*
>   or 4 *frying peppers, seeded and coarsely chopped*
> 1 *medium onion, coarsely chopped*
> 3 *medium tomatoes, peeled and chopped*
> 4 *sprigs parsley, chopped fine*
> 6 *or 7 fresh basil leaves, chopped fine or 1/2 tsp. dried
>   leaves*
> 1 *tsp. dried oregano leaves, crumbled*
> *salt and black pepper to taste*

Remove the stem end from the eggplants and discard. Cut the
unpeeled eggplants into less than bite-size cubes. Put flour
and salt in a plastic bag and shake to mix. Put a large skillet

over a medium flame to heat while you toss the eggplant cubes in the bag, holding the top tightly shut. Cover the bottom of the now hot skillet with oil and fry the flour-coated eggplant for about 5 minutes, turning constantly so all cubes are evenly, though only partially, cooked. Remove the skillet from the heat and with a slotted spoon transfer the eggplant to a large, shallow, oiled casserole, making an even layer of cubes to cover the bottom of the dish.

If you are using zucchini, prepare it next. Dice, coat and fry exactly as you did the eggplant. Zucchini requires less cooking time than eggplant—3 minutes of stir-frying will be quite enough. Arrange a layer of zucchini on top of the eggplant.

Wipe out the skillet and reheat. Cover the bottom with oil and stir-fry the peppers and onions for 2 minutes. Add the tomatoes and herbs. Reduce the heat and simmer a few minutes. Stir, taste, and add salt and pepper as required. Stir and pour over the vegetable cubes in the casserole.

Bake at 350° about 25 minutes or until the juices are bubbling. If the tomatoes are on the dry side, which may well be the case if you use an Italian plum type, moisten the casserole with tomato juice or plain water. I've tried both beef and chicken stock and found that each gave a dark, heavy taste which was at odds with the fresh, light flavors of the vegetables.

If, after baking, the texture is too soupy, sprinkle the top of the vegetables lightly with corn meal and return to the oven for 5 minutes. Remove the dish from the oven 5 minutes before serving time and drizzle with 1 jigger of good sherry. Some people like to sprinkle grated romano or parmesan cheese on *ratatouille*. Do serve it separately. Many people do not care for cheese with this dish. Accompany *ratatouille* with garlic bread, a big green salad and an egg entrée (Chapter 4) for a light, meatless and extremely economical lunch or light supper.

EGGPLANT SALAD

Sometimes called poor man's caviar, this is easy to prepare and has the virtue of being both pretty and different.

> 1 medium eggplant
> 2 tbsp. sesame paste
> juice of 2 lemons
> small clove of garlic, pressed
> 1/2 tsp. salt
> 1 tbsp. olive oil
> 3 sprigs parsley, very finely chopped
> 1 small red onion, thinly sliced

Toast the whole eggplant over the hibachi, barbecue grill or stove burner until the skin blackens and is about to burn. Cool the eggplant and peel off the skin. Dice the eggplant and mash thoroughly. A shallow wooden bowl and stainless steel pastry knife are ideal.

In the bottom of a bowl combine the sesame paste and lemon juice. Mash the garlic and salt together and add to the sesame paste. Mix well. The sauce should be thick but liquid. If it is too thick, add a spoonful of water. Mix the eggplant thoroughly with the sauce and pour it into a shallow bowl to serve. Make a pool of the olive oil in the center; surround it with a ring of chopped parsley and then a ring of red onion slices. This is a good dip for wheat or sesame seed crackers.

STRAWBERRIES

Through most of the United States strawberries begin to ripen in June—just in time to provide festive concoctions for bridal showers, brunches and graduation parties. The season is short, so make the most of it by having strawberries as often as you can in a variety of ways. If you grow your own, you can extend the season by planting early, midseason and late varieties. Unless you and your family are untiring strawberry devotées and have the time to tend three separate beds, it may be best to grow just one top quality variety that is suited to your area. Eat your fill for about three weeks, freeze some berries, convert some into jam and sauce, and then give strawberries a rest as peaches, melons and summer apples begin to ripen.

There are many old stories about the curative properties of the strawberry—especially in connection with pulmonary problems and gout. One such tale credits a strawberry diet with curing the gout of the great botanist Linnaeus. Today's tales tend to run more to allergies, and some people suffer unpleasant reactions to strawberries. A central Pennsylvania saying claims that indigestion from eating strawberries can be avoided by sprinkling the berries with ground cayenne pepper. It might be worth a try. For those unfortunates whose reaction takes the form of angry rashes and hives, the only solution is abstinence.

If your strawberries come from the country roadside stands or markets, buy ten quarts at a time to make the trip worthwhile. Use two quarts fresh in a day or two; preserve the remaining eight quarts in freezer packs, or as sauce or jam.

There are several simple ways of serving strawberries that are ideal for the first of the season and for when you have exceptionally fine, beautiful specimens. Simplest of all is to arrange the unhulled strawberries in a pyramid on a serving plate and supply each diner with a small bowl of honey or sugar. Hold the strawberries by their caps, dip and eat.

STRAWBERRIES SLICED AND SUGARED

Strawberries should be prepared an hour before serving so that the sugar has time to permeate the fruit. Drizzle orange juice over the sliced, sugared berries—especially early varieties that may tend to be low on flavor—to bring out the strawberry taste. Serve sugared strawberries alone or with cream, ice cream, waffles, or all three.

STRAWBERRIES IN CHAMPAGNE

These are elegant enough to serve at a wedding breakfast or brunch and are quick to prepare—a virtue that has particular appeal in the graduation and wedding season. Select the ripest and most perfect berries. Roll them gently in sugar and arrange in individual dishes. Sprinkle with champagne and chill for 30 minutes before serving. One quart of berries will serve 4 very generously, 6 quite adequately.

STRAWBERRY MOUSSE

This is a good way to use ripe berries that are less than perfect.

> 1 qt. ripe strawberries, hulled
> 3/4 cup sugar, approximate
> 1-2/3 cups evaporated milk, chilled
> 2 tbsp. lemon juice

Put a 6 cup mold or refrigerator trays in the refrigerator to chill. Press the strawberries through a coarse sieve or purée them briefly in the blender. The result will be about 2 cups of pulp and juice. Stir the sugar into the pulp and taste. Add a little more sugar if the mixture is still too tart. Whip the chilled milk until it is very stiff; fold in the lemon juice and strawberry mixture. Pour into the mold or trays at once and freeze until firm (about 2 hours). This serves 6 nicely.

STRAWBERRIES AND CREAM MOLD

This is a good deal richer than the mousse.

4 tsp. unflavored gelatin
1/4 cup cold water
2 cups cream
1/4 cup sugar
1 cup sour cream
1 pt. strawberries
1/4 cup honey or sugar

Soak the gelatin in the cold water. Meanwhile combine the cream and 1/4 cup sugar, and heat to scalding (until a skin forms on top) but do not allow to boil. Stir the gelatin and water mixture into the hot cream until it is completely dissolved. Chill this mixture until it begins to thicken, stirring occasionally. When thick, fold in the sour cream until the mixture is smooth. Turn into a buttered quart mold and chill until firm. If you prepare this right after lunch, it is sure to be firm by dinnertime.

Hull and crush the strawberries and sweeten with the honey or sugar. At serving time, unmold the cream on a chilled serving dish and pour the strawberries over it. I give this recipe for 8 servings since it is usually prepared when company comes. You can, of course, halve it and use a pint mold to serve 4.

STRAWBERRY SHERBET

This is a rich sherbet—not the low calorie, water-ice variety.

1-1/2 cups milk
1 cup sugar
1-1/2 cups strawberries
1/4 cup lemon juice
3 egg whites
1 cup heavy cream

Chill a mixing bowl for whipping the egg whites.

Heat the milk slightly and stir in sugar until it dissolves. Cool the mixture, then partially freeze it. Press the strawberries through a sieve fine enough to remove the seeds. Turn the half-frozen milk into a cold bowl and beat smooth; fold in the strawberry pulp and lemon juice. Pour into freezer trays and partially freeze. Beat the egg whites in the chilled bowl until they form stiff peaks. Whip the cream and combine it with the egg whites. Turn the berry mixture into a cold bowl and beat briefly to soften. Fold in the cream mixture and freeze until firm.

STRAWBERRY ICE CREAM—NEAPOLITAN STYLE

1-1/2 cups light cream
3/4 cup sugar
dash of salt—scant 1/4 tsp.
4 egg yolks
2 cups heavy cream
1-1/2 cups strawberries, hulled and slightly crushed

Scald the light cream in the top pan of a double boiler. Do not let it boil. Stir in the sugar and salt to dissolve. Beat the egg yolks in a bowl, blend a little of the hot cream into the yolks, and then gradually pour the yolks into the cream. Put the pan over hot water (bottom pan of double boiler) and cook, stirring constantly, until the mixture thickens into a custard. Remove from heat, let cool, and fold in heavy cream and strawberries. Pour into the can of the ice cream churn and turn till stiff.

STRAWBERRY ICE CREAM—PHILADELPHIA STYLE

1 pt. strawberries
1 cup sugar
1 pt. milk
1 pt. cream

1 *tbsp. lemon juice*
pinch of salt

Hull and mash the berries and stir in the sugar. Let sit 30 minutes. Add the milk, cream, lemon juice and salt. Mix well and taste. Add sugar if needed. Pour into freezer can and freeze.

STRAWBERRY SHORTCAKE

Several times in strawberry season, especially when Jersey Belles are at their peak, I throw the balanced diet and calorie counting out the window and make a whole meal of strawberry shortcake. This country version of a classic American dessert comes to me from Pennsylvania through my mother's family. When the berries are lush and fragrant, the whipped cream real and the biscuits hot from the oven, this dish is near perfection.

2 *qts. strawberries*
sugar to taste—usually 1-1/2 to 2 cups
1-1/2 *cups whipping cream*

About 2 hours before shortcake time, hull and slice the strawberries into a large bowl. Sugar them to taste and let them sit, turning occasionally, while they become sweet and juicy. Half an hour before serving time put the bowl for whipping the cream and the beaters in the refrigerator to chill. Mix up the biscuits and put in the oven. Five minutes before the biscuits are done, whip the cream.

BAKING POWDER BISCUITS

2 *cups flour*
4 *tsp. baking powder*
1 *tsp. salt*
2 *tbsp. sugar*
2 *tbsp. shortening*
3/4 *cup milk, approximate*

Mix flour, baking powder, salt and sugar, and sift together twice. Cut the shortening in with 2 knives or blender. Mix in milk gradually to make a soft dough. Sometimes you may need a little more milk. Roll out dough on a floured board to 1/2 inch thick and cut with a biscuit cutter or the top of a juice glass. Arrange the rounds of dough on a greased baking sheet and bake at 450° for 12 to 15 minutes, removing when the biscuits begin to brown on top.

Give each person a good-size soup bowl. Put the bowls of strawberries and whipped cream and a basket of hot biscuits on the table and let everyone make his own. This works very well, since some like more or less of berries or cream, and it saves jumping up and down to fix second helpings. You can add a bowl of vanilla ice cream in a bed of ice. If you do, it should be hand dipped, preferably homemade.

STRAWBERRY SAUCE

This is a lovely luxury to have on hand through the winter. Pour it over waffles, pancakes or French toast at breakfast; use it for dessert waffles, sundaes, milkshakes and strawberry water ice for children.

> *strawberries (8 qts. berries will yield 5 to 7 pts. sauce)*
> *sugar (1 cup to each 2 pounds of berry purée)*

Purée the hulled strawberries in the blender or press through a medium sieve. Add 1 cup sugar to each 2 pounds purée and stir well to dissolve. Fill pint or half-pint jars and seal. Process 6 minutes in boiling water; turn off heat and let the jars cool in the kettle. When cool, remove from the water, wipe the jars, and tighten the rings if necessary. Store in a cool, dark place.

If you have freezer space to spare, you can freeze this sauce, but it is not then ready for use instantly.

Freezing strawberries. Select 4 quarts of ripe, sound berries to yield 6 pints of frozen berries. Hull the berries and slice them into a bowl. Add 3 cups sugar and mix with the berries until sugar is dissolved and some juice appears. Pack the berries in pint freezer containers leaving half an inch of head space. Crumple a piece of freezer paper and put it on top of the berries so that when the lid is put on, they will be pressed down in the juice. Put on the lid, making sure it is firmly sealed, and freeze.

Be sure to label strawberries, since frozen tomato gravy, rhubarb and cherries are sometimes difficult to distinguish from berries through the frosted sides of plastic containers.

PEACHES

August and early September is the height of the peach season. Roadside stands and farmers' markets often sell peaches by the basket rather than by the pound. In my area two-, four-, eight- and sixteen-quart baskets are the rule. The best buy for a small family is often the four-quart basket which holds about 40 peaches and weighs from eight to ten pounds. Pick out the best peaches for eating out of hand and for fresh peach desserts. Bake, can or freeze the rest, or put up jam, preserves, marmalade or chutney.

The Spanish conquistadors are credited with introducing the peach to this continent when they planted the first trees in Florida before 1600. Today there are many varieties, and the late ripening types extend the season to early October. The difference that most concerns the cook is whether the peach in question is a freestone or cling type. A general rule is that freestone types have very fuzzy skins and juicy flesh; clings are less fuzzy and have firmer flesh.

Almost all recipes require that peaches be peeled. To peel

ripe peaches most smoothly and easily and with the least waste, dip them into boiling water, then into cold water, and peel at once.

Next to eating out of hand, sliced and sugared peaches are simplest. To effect a subtle difference, sweeten the peaches with honey to which a drop of almond extract has been added. This makes a nice instant syrup with the peach juice.

PEACHES IN SAUTERNE

This is a refreshing, austere dessert to follow a rich summer dinner.

1 peach for each diner
sauterne

Peel and slice peaches carefully into a deep bowl. Cover them with sauterne and let stand about 15 minutes, undisturbed. Ladle peaches into individual bowls and drizzle *very* lightly with honey. Strain the sauterne, which will now be slightly peach flavored, and serve a small glass of the wine with each bowl of fruit.

PEACH MELBA

This attractive and delicious dessert is easily and quickly fixed, provided you have ice cream on hand and remember to remove the raspberries from the freezer in time.

1/2 pt. vanilla ice cream
2 peaches (1/2 for each diner), peeled
1/2 pt. frozen raspberries, thawed
   or 1/2 pt. raspberry purée or syrup (p. 174)

Put a layer of vanilla ice cream in the bottom of each dessert dish, place a peeled pitted peach half on the ice cream, and spoon raspberries over the peach. Serve at once.

GRILLED PEACHES

These are an interesting accompaniment to certain meat dishes—especially baked ham, roast pork and duck. Peel, pit and halve 4 ripe peaches. Brush the cut sides with butter, coat with sugar and put a dab of butter in the seed cavity. Broil the peach halves until they glaze. Sprinkle with lemon juice or vinegar and arrange around roast.

BAKED PEACHES

This is a simple dessert, lighter than a two-crust pie, and easy enough for a young beginning cook to make with a minimum of supervision and risk.

> 1 *cup sugar*
> 1 *cup flour*
> 1/2 *tsp. salt*
> 1/2 *tsp. baking powder*
> 1/2 *cup butter*
> 1 *egg, beaten*
> 4 *peaches, peeled*
> 1 *tbsp. lemon juice*

Sift sugar, flour, salt and baking powder together. Blend in butter. Add the egg and mix well. Slice the peaches into a baking dish and sprinkle with the lemon juice. Spread the dough over the peaches and bake at 375° for 30 to 40 minutes or until nicely browned on top. Serve with a pitcher of cream at room temperature.

PEACHES IN BED

1 lb. graham crackers
1/4 lb. butter, softened
2 lbs. peaches, peeled
2 small packages cream cheese
2 tbsp. confectioners sugar
1/4 tsp. vanilla
1 cup sour cream (may need a little more)

Crush the crackers and work the butter into them. Spread this mixture evenly on the bottom and sides of a deep pie dish to form a shell. Bake about 7 minutes at 350°. Let cool. Slice the peaches into the crumb shell. Combine the cream cheese, sugar and vanilla. Add sour cream until the mixture becomes soft enough to spread with ease over the peaches. Chill thoroughly and serve.

The next three peach delicacies are not generally available commercially. They are nice to have in your own pantry and they make wonderfully personal and different gifts. Peach Marmalade and Peach Leather are especially popular with children. Peach Chutney is a more adult treat.

PEACH MARMALADE

11 peaches, peeled
2 oranges
sugar
10 maraschino cherries

Quarter the peaches and oranges. Remove the seeds from the oranges but do not peel. Put both fruits through the medium blade of the food mill. If you like a sweeter marmalade, add one cup sugar for each cup of fruit and juice.

If you prefer a slightly tart taste, reduce the sugar to 3/4 cup per cup of fruit.

Boil the fruit slowly, stirring frequently, for about 45 minutes, or until the bits of orange peel are cooked through. Dice the maraschino cherries and stir into the fruit. Ladle into hot sterilized jars and seal. Let stand about a month before beginning to use.

PEACH LEATHER

This ancient confection was devised long before freezers and mason jars. It is very similar to the rolled sheets of dried apricots that are sold in restaurants featuring Middle Eastern cooking.

Peel very ripe peaches and press the pulp through a sieve until you have 2 quarts of pulp in a saucepan. Stir in 1 pint of brown sugar. Boil for 2 minutes. Let cool; spread the mixture on a slab of marble or wood, and put it in the sun daily until the paste leaves the slab readily. If the air and sun in your vicinity are something less than Mediterranean in quality, it is best to dry the paste in a very slow oven.

Dust the top of the dry paste with sugar, sandwich it between two pieces of wax paper and roll up. Store in a dry place.

PEACH CHUTNEY

Excellent with any curry, ham or pork dishes. Visitors here often eat chutnies with omelettes and baked beans.

> 3-1/2 lbs. ripe peaches, peeled
> 1 cup cider vinegar
> 1 lb. dark brown sugar
> 1 medium onion, grated
> 1 lb. raisins
> 3 apples, cored, pared and diced
> 1 tbsp. white mustard seed
> 1/2 cup scraped ginger root
> 3 tsp. salt
> 1 tbsp. paprika
> 1 tsp. cumin
> grated rind and juice of 1 lemon

Dice the peaches into a large bowl. Add the vinegar and brown sugar and mix.

In a large, heavy saucepan combine the onion, raisins, apples, mustard seed, ginger root, salt, paprika, cumin, and lemon rind and juice. Cook this mixture over a low to medium flame. Stir it constantly and do not look away from it for a moment. The object of cooking such an essentially dry mixture is to "cure" the spices, to mellow the flavor of the cumin, mustard and ginger.

When the mixture seems on the point of scorching, remove it from the heat and toss a couple of ice cubes into the pan to stop the cooking process at once.

Now cook the sugared peaches separately until they are tender. Add the peaches to the spice mixture and cook 5 minutes, stirring constantly. Ladle into hot jars and seal.

Yield: About 6 pints.

PEACH SAUCE

This is good served hot over waffles, puddings or ice cream. It's good for using up the few odd peaches left over from canning or preserving. If you have enough peaches on hand, make a double recipe and freeze half for cold weather breakfasts.

1/3 cup sugar
1 tbsp. cornstarch
1/4 tsp. salt
1/2 cup boiling water
1 tbsp. lemon juice
1/2 tsp. grated lemon rind
1 cup crushed peaches
1 cup sliced peaches

Combine sugar, cornstarch and salt. Gradually stir in the water and cook until the mixture thickens, stirring constantly. Add lemon juice, rind and crushed peaches. Simmer for 5 minutes. Add sliced peaches and simmer 5 minutes. Serve hot at once or freeze.

BRANDIED PEACHES

Scald, peel and weigh ripe, unbruised peaches. For each pound of fruit measure 1 cup sugar and 1 cup water into a saucepan. Boil sugar and water to make a syrup; add the peaches a few at a time and boil them until they are slightly soft (about 5 minutes). Pack the peaches as they are ready into hot sterilized jars. Fill the jars 1/2 to 3/4 full of hot syrup, and fill to the top with *good* brandy and seal. Do not open for at least 90 days.

PEACH PRESERVES

2 *lbs. peaches, peeled*
3 *cups sugar*
2 *cups water*
3 *drops almond extract*

Slice peaches. Boil sugar and water together for 2 minutes. Let syrup cool. Add the peaches and cook until peaches are translucent. Let cool for 3 hours. Ladle the cool peaches into hot jars, using a slotted spoon. Add almond extract and boil the syrup until it thickens. Pour the hot syrup over the fruit and fill jars to within 1/2 inch of the top. Seal and store.

Yield: About 2 pints.

Peaches can be canned or frozen using a variety of methods. Peaches are most economically packed in water, but tend to lose a good deal of their flavor and color. Water pack is only an immediate economy since when you use the peaches, they will require sugar. For the many methods, advantages and instruction for putting up peaches, see *The Complete Book of Home Preserving* by Anne Seranne (New York: Doubleday & Co., 1955). The recipe which follows produces a fruit which is ready to use "as is" for a quick dessert, in pies, ice cream, puddings or sauces.

CANNED PEACHES IN MEDIUM SYRUP

3 *cups sugar*
6 *cups water*
10 *lbs. peaches*

Boil the sugar and water together for 5 minutes. Peel, pit and slice the peaches. Cook them gently in the syrup until just tender. Ladle them into hot jars with the syrup, filling the jars to within 1/2 inch of the top. Seal and process in boiling water—20 minutes for both pint and quart jars.

Yield: About 10 pints.

Freezing peaches. Peel about 8 pounds of peaches. Combine 3 cups sugar and 4 cups water and stir to dissolve. You can use hot water or cook slightly to save stirring time. Try to make the syrup sufficiently ahead of time to have it cool when you pack the fruit in freezer containers. Pour about 1/3 cup cold syrup into each freezer container. Slice the peaches directly into container in order to handle as little as possible. Cover the fruit with more syrup. Put a piece of crumpled freezer paper on top of the peaches so all will be submerged in the syrup. Put on the lid, seal firmly and freeze.

CHAPTER 3

Staple Standbys and Winter Keepers

I WORK, and play, hard in winter—cutting wood, mending fence, ice skating, sledding. Frequent guests take part in these activities and all hands are hungry most of the time. To eat heartily, economically and well without spending all day in the kitchen, I rely on staples that can cook slowly with a minimum of attention all day, and on quickly fixed dishes whose precooking requirements can largely be accomplished the night before.

The big three of winter staples in my kitchen are beans, rice and pasta. By the end of September the pantry is well stocked with dried lima, pea, pinto, kidney and black beans. Homemade bean dishes are a gourmet delight to those of us (a majority, I fear) whose only bean experience has been via the can opener. A fragrant casserole of barbecued limas is difficult to resist. Such a dish becomes the backbone of the meal and diverts attention from the meat-stretching nature of the entrée.

BEANS

All these bean recipes will serve four persons generously. Any leftovers, delicious warmed up, will disappear at lunch the following day. Young guests here even make bean sandwiches on hamburger rolls.

BAKED BEANS

Good year-round, baked beans hit the spot especially on cold winter evenings.

> 2 *cups pea beans, washed and picked over*
> 6 *thick strips of good bacon*
> 1 *medium onion, chopped*
> 3/4 *cup dark brown sugar*
> 2 *tsp. salt*
> 1/2 *tsp. dry mustard*
> 1/4 *tsp. ground cloves*
> 2 *tbsp. ketchup*

Bring the beans to boil in plenty of water. Do not cover the pot or they will boil over the minute your back is turned. Let boil briskly 2 minutes, then reduce heat and simmer until the beans are tender—about 1 hour. Bite a bean to test it. If it breaks apart easily between your teeth, it is tender. Further simmering will make beans mushy and too much like canned beans.

While the beans are simmering, dice the raw bacon and spread it evenly on the bottom of a 2-quart bean pot or casserole. Spread the diced onion on the bacon. With a slotted spoon, ladle the beans into the pot. Heat 2 cups of the water the beans cooked in and add to it all the remaining ingredients, stirring well. Pour enough of this mixture over the beans to cover them. Save the rest of the bean liquid to add to the beans if they get too dry while baking or to moisten them, should they need it, when they are reheated. Cover the pot or casserole and bake at 250° for 7 hours. Uncover the pot for the last hour of baking so the beans on top form a brown crust.

BARBECUED LIMA BEANS

2 *cups dried lima beans, washed*
3 *tbsp. bacon drippings*
1 *medium onion, minced*
1 *clove garlic, minced*
1 *tbsp. Worcestershire sauce*
2 *tbsp. prepared mustard*
1 *tsp. chili powder*
1 *pt. canned tomatoes*
1 *tbsp. flour*
1 *tbsp. sugar*
1/4 *cup vinegar*
2 *tsp. salt*

Soak the beans 1 hour in cold water. Bring to boil in fresh water, reduce heat and simmer until tender—from 30 minutes to 1 hour.

Heat a large skillet, put in bacon drippings, and sauté the onion and garlic until they are soft. Add remaining ingredients and simmer, stirring from time to time, until well blended. Add beans and stir well. Pour beans into a 2-quart casserole and add bean liquid to cover. Save the rest of the bean water to add if needed during baking. Bake, uncovered, at 350° for 1 hour.

RANCH-STYLE BEANS

These and Refried Beans (next recipe) are well known in Texas and Arizona and deserve to be better known everywhere.

2 cups *pinto beans, washed*
2 *medium onions, diced*
2 *cloves garlic, diced*
1 *can (3-1/2 oz.) roasted green chiles, if you like them
    and if you have them*
1 *pt. canned tomatoes*
1 *tsp. cumin seed, ground or crushed in mortar*
1 *tsp. chili powder*
2 *tsp. salt*

Bring beans to boil in 2 quarts of water. Reduce heat and simmer until tender (about 1 hour). Add diced onion and garlic, chiles, tomatoes, cumin and chili powder. Simmer for an hour and a half, stirring occasionally and adding just enough water to keep beans covered if needed. Ten minutes before serving, add salt and stir well.

REFRIED BEANS

A loaf-shaped platter of *refritos*, a pile of yellow rice (p. 69), fried chicken and a salad make a warming, filling winter lunch.

2 cups *kidney beans or pinto beans, washed*
1 *medium onion, diced*
1 *clove garlic, diced*
3 *tbsp. bacon drippings*
1 *tsp. chili powder*
2 *tsp. salt*

Soak beans 1 hour in cold water and bring to boil. Reduce heat and add onion and garlic and simmer until beans are tender, about 45 minutes. Heat a large skillet and melt bacon drippings. With a slotted spoon, transfer some beans to the skillet. Mash the beans with a potato masher, push to the edge of the skillet and repeat, occasionally adding some bean liquid, until all the beans have been mashed. Add about 1 cup of the bean liquid, the chili powder and salt and mix thoroughly with the beans. The consistency should be that of a very thick soup. Cook and stir until the mixture begins to dry and is the consistency of mashed potatoes. Pat into a loaf form on a heated platter and serve.

If you can't manage cooking and mashing in the same pan at the same time, mash the beans in a separate dish or put them briefly in the blender. I would rather take more time to mash the beans by hand than to wash the blender.

CLIO'S KIDNEY BEANS

The brown sugar and hickory smoked salt give these a different savor. If you have liquid smoke on hand, use 1/4 teaspoon of it with 2 teaspoons plain salt instead of hickory smoked salt.

> 2 *cups kidney beans, washed*
> 1 *medium onion, diced*
> 2 *slices bacon, diced*
> 1 *green pepper, seeded and diced*
> 1/2 *pt. canned tomatoes*
> 2 *tbsp. brown sugar*
> 2 *tsp. hickory smoked salt*

Bring kidney beans to a boil, then simmer until tender. Add remaining ingredients and simmer very slowly about 4 hours, adding more water if necessary.

COUNTRY-STYLE BEANS

> 2 *cups pea beans*
> 2 *tsp. salt*
> 1 *clove garlic, minced*

1 *bay leaf*
4 *strips bacon, diced*
1 *medium onion, diced*
1 *green pepper, chopped*
1/2 *pt. canned tomatoes*
1/4 *cup parsley, chopped*
1/2 *tsp. oregano*

Bring beans to boil, then simmer until tender. Leave enough water to cover and add salt, garlic and bay leaf; continue to simmer. Fry the bacon, remove with a slotted spoon and add to beans. Sauté the onion in the bacon fat until soft; then add pepper, tomatoes, parsley and oregano. Mix well, stir mixture into beans and simmer 2 hours.

BEAN SOUP

A meal-in-itself kind of soup. Serve with sandwiches or garlic bread and a salad.

2 *cups pea beans or limas, washed*
1 *hambone with some meat left on it*
2 *medium potatoes, boiled, peeled and puréed*
1 *medium onion, diced*
1/2 *cup celery, diced*
1/2 *pt. tomatoes, puréed*
salt and pepper to taste

Bring beans to boil, reduce heat and simmer for 30 minutes. Add enough water to make 5 quarts of liquid in the soup pot. Simmer until beans are easily mashed. Add all remaining ingredients except salt. Put a lid on the pot and simmer soup 1 hour. Remove the hambone, shred the meat and put it in the soup. Salt to taste and serve. This recipe makes 8 large servings; if you are only feeding 4 people, freeze 2 quarts.

BLACK BEAN SOUP

This recipe is for 4 servings, since I do not care for this soup reheated or frozen.

1 heaping cup black beans, washed
1 small to medium onion, diced
1 small stalk celery, diced
1/2 cup lean ham, diced fine
1 tbsp. vinegar
1 clove garlic, diced
1/8 tsp. cayenne pepper
salt to taste
3 tbsp. good sherry
1 medium onion, chopped very fine
1 cup steamed rice (p. 65)

Simmer beans in 3 quarts water. Add the onion and celery and cook until beans are well cooked. Purée beans in blender or put through a medium sieve. Reduce the bean water to 2 quarts or add water if necessary. Add bean purée, ham, vinegar, garlic and cayenne, and salt to taste. Simmer about 20 minutes. When ready to serve, remove from heat and stir in sherry. Garnish with finely chopped onion and serve with a bowl of rice.

BEAN SALAD

1 cup pea or marrow beans, washed
1/4 cup olive oil or peanut oil
1 tbsp. vinegar
1 tsp. salt
1 tbsp. onion, very finely chopped
2 tbsp. parsley, very finely chopped
1/4 tsp. marjoram

Bring beans to boil, reduce heat and simmer until tender. Combine and mix the remaining ingredients in a deep bowl.

With a slotted spoon, ladle the hot beans into the marinade and let sit at room temperature 1 hour, stirring occasionally. Serve in the bowl or heaped on a small platter. You can enrich this salad by garnishing with quartered hardboiled eggs or flaked tuna fish, or both. This recipe makes 4 servings.

RICE

Here are the six rice recipes I use most. Do not substitute any instant, or even quick, product for the real thing. I buy white short-grain rice and brown natural rice in 25-pound bags in fall, and store it in lard tins in the pantry. If you use rice fairly frequently, buy it in bulk—both for economy's sake and for the pleasant certainty that you always have rice on hand. The brown rice is nice to use when you are using plain rice as a vegetable.

Cooking rice. So many people say "I have bad luck with rice" or "I'm never sure how rice will turn out," that to give a basic recipe for cooking plain rice seems a good idea. I nearly always make 2 cups since leftover rice has so many uses. To serve two people with little or nothing left over, halve the recipe.

> 2 *cups rice*
> 2 *cups water*
> 1 *tsp. peanut oil, optional*
> 1 *tsp. salt, optional*

Wash the rice in two changes of water, rubbing the grains through your fingers and draining thoroughly each time. Put 2 cups water in a heavy saucepan that has a close-fitting lid. Add the rice (and the oil and salt, if you are going to use them) and bring to a boil. Let boil quite briskly for 1 minute. Give one last stir to make sure nothing is sticking to the bottom, clamp on the lid, reduce the heat at once to very low and let cook 15 minutes undisturbed. Do not stir, prod, or even peek. After 15 minutes, lift the lid. If the surface of the rice is dotted with little craters, it is probably done. Taste a couple of the grains on top. "Very low" heat may differ from stove to stove. If you have to cook the rice longer than 15 minutes, make a note of the time required, for next time. Then you can turn off the heat 5 minutes ahead of time— the rice will continue to steam if you do not uncover it. This method unfailingly produces well-cooked, firm, separate grains of rice.

FRIED RICE

This recipe serves 4, and does not reheat well.

1 large onion, coarsely chopped
1 clove garlic, sliced
1 stalk celery, coarsely chopped
peanut oil to cover bottom of skillet
1 can bean sprouts (16 oz.), drained
1 cup cooked rice
1 tbsp. soy sauce
salt to taste
1 egg, optional

Heat a large skillet and stir-fry onion, garlic and celery in oil 2 minutes. Vegetables should be crisp and just barely cooked. Quickly add the bean sprouts, rice and soy sauce. Stir-fry lightly until all ingredients are mixed and heated through. Taste and add salt and more soy sauce if needed. If you like egg with fried rice, clear a spot in the center of the skillet, break an egg on it, scramble with a fork until it is dry and crumbly, mix with rice and serve at once.

If you make fried rice in summer, you can replace the bean sprouts with fresh vegetables. In late spring use chop suey greens or snow peas or both. Through summer use the chopped ribs of Swiss chard, shaved green cabbage and chopped green pepper. From mid-September to early November Chinese cabbage (Bok Choy or Pak Choy) is plentiful. Chop it fine for fried rice and use plenty, since its bulk diminishes dramatically as it cooks.

CURRIED RICE

This dry curry, not so well known in this country as curried chicken, grows on people. If you eat it often, you will probably find your curry getting stronger and stronger. Remember that guests may be first-time curry eaters, and measure spices accordingly. This recipe is mild. The rice with its sauces and chutnies is the center of any meal and is nicely accompanied by chicken—baked or broiled—and a cool cucumber or tomato salad.

> 1 *tbsp. oil*
> 2 *medium onions, coarsely chopped*
> 2 *cloves garlic, sliced*
> 2 *slices ginger, chopped*
> 2 *tbsp. curry powder (preferably homemade, p. 165)*
> *or 2 tbsp. garam masala for a sweet, unpiquant curry (p. 166)*
> 2 *cups water*
> 2 *tsp. salt*
> 1 *bay leaf*
> 2 *cups rice, washed and drained*

Heat a heavy-bottom stainless steel saucepan (if you cook this often in tin or aluminum, the metal will soon become badly pitted) that has a tight-fitting lid. Put in oil and fry onion, garlic and ginger until they begin to soften. Have the 2 cups water at hand. Add the curry powder to the saucepan and stir and cook, watching very carefully. When the mixture seems on the point of burning, pour in the water to stop the cooking at once. Add salt, bay leaf and washed rice. Cook, stirring carefully to be sure nothing is sticking to the bottom.

Bring rapidly to a boil, stir one last time, put lid on securely, lower heat to very low and let rice cook 15 minutes. Do not lift lid. If holes have appeared in the rice, it is probably done to your taste. Try a few grains on top. If it is just a little too firm, put the lid back on quickly and let the rice continue to steam in its pot without bottom heat.

While the rice is steaming, make 2 sauces.

PINK SAUCE

> 1 tbsp. olive oil
> 1 tsp. black mustard seed, crushed in mortar
> 1 tsp. coriander seed, crushed in mortar
> 2 tbsp. tomato paste
> 3 tbsp. sour cream
> water to thin, as needed

Heat oil in a small saucepan; add black mustard seed and coriander, put lid on so seeds don't spatter about, and cook 1 minute over a medium flame. Remove from the fire and, when seeds have stopped popping, remove lid. Stir in tomato paste and sour cream. Thin sauce with water so that it is liquid. Do not salt. Return to the stove and let simmer about 10 minutes while you make the second sauce.

WHITE SAUCE

Make this in the last 5 minutes rice is cooking so onions are fresh and crisp.

> 2 medium onions
> juice of 1 lemon
> 1 pt. plain yogurt

Dice or grate the onions very fine. Add onions and lemon juice to the yogurt; mix well and pour into serving bowl. This sauce should be dense with onion. The effect, strangely enough, is cooling when eaten with the curry.

Put the hot pan of rice on a trivet on the table. Surround it with bowls of the sauces, chutnies, chopped peanuts, etc.— as many of the traditional curry accompaniments as you care for.

Have tissues at hand—the curry, mild as this is, will clear sinuses and make noses run.

PILAU

There are endless variations of pilau, as there are of risotto. This is a very plain, standard pilau that goes so well with lamb and pork dishes.

1/4 lb. butter
2 tbsp. olive oil
1 medium onion, chopped fine
1 clove garlic, diced
1/4 tsp. ground cloves
2 cups rice, washed and drained
1 tsp. salt
1-3/4 cups boiling water
1/4 cup raisins, soaked 2 hours in water
1/4 cup toasted almonds, chopped coarsely

Melt the butter and oil in a heavy pan; add onion, garlic and clove powder. Cook until the onion is soft. Add rice and salt; cook and stir about 3 minutes. Add boiling water and raisins. Cover pan tightly and cook very slowly 25 to 30 minutes, when all the liquid will have been absorbed and rice will be tender. Turn out on a heated platter and garnish with the almonds.

YELLOW RICE

This goes well served or mixed with either cooked green peas or country-style beans (p. 62).

> 1 tbsp. oil
> 1 bay leaf
> 1 tsp. salt
> 1/2 tsp. saffron, ground and soaked in 1 tbsp. water
> 2 cups rice, washed and drained
> 2 cups water

Put oil in a heavy saucepan and tilt so bottom and sides are coated. Heating will make oil more fluid. Add bay leaf, salt, saffron, rice and water. Bring to a brisk boil, stirring constantly. Put the lid on tightly, reduce heat, and cook 15 to 20 minutes until rice is tender. Remove bay leaf, which will be on top of the rice, and serve.

RICE PUDDING

Make this in time to serve hot with cream. Thaw some peach sauce (p. 55) to heat and serve with the pudding.

> 1 qt. milk
> 1/4 cup rice, washed
> 1/2 tsp. salt
> 1/2 cup sugar
> 1/2 tsp. nutmeg, grated
> 1/4 tsp. vanilla
> 1/2 cup raisins, soaked 2 hours in warm water (optional)

Mix milk, rice, salt and sugar in a 1-1/2-quart casserole or baking dish. Bake at 300° for 2 hours, stirring every half hour. Add nutmeg, vanilla and raisins, and stir. Bake undisturbed until rice is tender—45 minutes to 1 hour.

PASTA

In my growing-up years the only pasta I knew at home was elbow macaroni in macaroni and cheese. By the end of the twelfth grade I had discovered the world of pasta. *Linguine aglio-olio* (p. 72), still cheap today but practically free fifteen years ago, sustained my roommate and me through the hungriest of our college days. Now I eat pasta in some form about four times a week—from preference as well as economy.

Dieters, if they are not extremists, can eat pasta. The trouble is that we associate spaghetti and meat balls and kindred dishes with orgies of overeating. "She made lasagne. Boy, did I stuff myself." "There was ravioli, spaghetti—I ate till I couldn't move." We have all heard similar paeans. If someone at your table is watching his weight, cook a limited amount of pasta—sufficient for one serving apiece—and let it go at that. Unless one performs physical work or exercise, pasta should be eaten in the same proportion to the meal as any other vegetable.

Here are seven fast, stove-top pasta dishes. The sauce can be prepared while the pasta is cooking. There are also four oven-baked pasta casseroles, two substantial soups and two homemade pasta dishes that are especially good on cold winter days.

PASTA WITH TOMATO GRAVY

This is the classic Italian dish in America. It is quick to prepare only if you have the tomato gravy (p. 31), with or without the meatballs (p. 134), in the refrigerator, freezer or pantry. Do cook the pasta *al dente* and do cook easily managed forms such as *mostaccioli,* rigatoni or shells (*maruzze, conchigle*) if children or guests have not yet learned how to eat the long forms (spaghetti, *linguine, fusilli,* etc.) neatly. One pound of pasta will serve 4 generously, or should be divided among 6 dieters. One pint of tomato gravy is sufficient for 1 pound of pasta—at least according to most Italian tastes. Many Americans prefer more gravy—you have to make your own rule of thumb.

LINGUINE AGLIO-OLIO

This cheap, simple, rather crude dish does not appeal to everyone. The first time I tasted it, I thought it dreadful. Some weeks later I had a yen to taste it again. This time I polished off a full soup bowl with ease and mopped up the sauce with bread. Try half a recipe if you have never had *aglio-olio* before.

> 1 *lb. linguine*
> *salt*
> 3 *tbsp. olive oil*
> 6 *cloves garlic, sliced*
> 1/2 *tsp. crushed red pepper*
> 2 *tbsp. (about 4 sprigs) parsley, very finely chopped*

Cook the linguine *al dente* in boiling, salted water. Heat a small skillet; put in olive oil and sauté garlic until it softens. Remove pan from heat and add the red pepper. Pour the well drained pasta into a hot bowl. Heat oil and garlic until garlic begins to brown; pour over pasta at once and add chopped parsley. Toss very thoroughly and serve. Put a bowl of grated cheese on the table. Tastes vary; I like cheese on the second helping only.

COMPANY AGLIO-OLIO

Everyone seems to like this except those few who don't care for fish in any form. It is *aglio-olio* slightly dressed up and slightly subdued.

> 1 *lb. linguine*
> *salt*
> 3 *tbsp. olive oil*
> 2 *cloves garlic, sliced*
> 4 *tbsp. sliced mushrooms, fresh or canned (I have used*

pickled mushrooms in a pinch—just rinse off as much
pickle flavor as you can.)
2 tbsp. tuna fish
 or 4 anchovy fillets, chopped
dash tabasco sauce
2 tbsp. (about 4 sprigs) parsley, chopped

Boil linguine *al dente* in plenty of salted water. Heat a
medium-size skillet, and put in oil and chopped garlic. Watch
closely. When garlic begins to shrink, remove from fire and
add mushrooms, fish and tabasco sauce. Drain cooked linguine
and pour the sauce over it; add parsley and toss well. The fish
is used here strictly as a condiment and should be inconspicuous when pasta has been well mixed.

SPAGHETTI WITH ONION AND BACON

This is surprisingly good—and a pleasant change for those
who tire of tomato-based sauces.

1 lb. spaghetti, spaghettini, fusilli or linguine
salt
8 slices bacon
1 medium onion
2 cloves garlic, sliced
3 tbsp. grated parmesan, romano, etc. cheese

Boil pasta in salted water. Meanwhile, cut bacon slices into
long thin strips, or shave 1/2 cup paper-thin strips from a
very cold or frozen piece of slab bacon. If you use shaved
bacon, sauté the onions and garlic first in just enough olive
oil to cover the bottom of a small skillet and add bacon when
onions begin to soften. If you cut the bacon strips with a
knife, cook the bacon first and sauté onion strips and garlic
in the bacon fat. To make strips of onions, peel and slice the
onion thinly; make one cut through each slice from the edge

to the center so that as they cook the onions will be in strings instead of rings—that is, the same form as the bacon and pasta. It's a little more trouble but well worth the effort. With pasta, bacon and onion in strips, all three can be picked up on the fork at once so that the quality of the dish is improved.

Drain the cooked pasta and turn into a heated bowl. Add the grated cheese. Toss well and serve immediately.

MACARONI WITH RICOTTA

You can use cottage cheese if you don't have ricotta. Taste the cottage cheese before you add it and reduce the salt measurement accordingly. Most commercial cottage cheese that I have tasted is a good deal saltier than ricotta.

> 1 *lb. pasta—egg noodles (fettuccine) are probably best*
> 1/2 *lb. ricotta cheese*
> 1/2 *tsp. salt*
> 1/4 *tsp. black pepper*
> 1/8 *tsp. nutmeg*
> 3 *tbsp. hot water*

Boil pasta *al dente* in salted water. While it is cooking combine the ricotta, salt, pepper and nutmeg in a bowl. Beat in the hot water until the mixture is smooth. Drain the cooked pasta well, turn into a hot serving dish, toss well with the ricotta sauce and serve with grated cheese.

FETTUCCINE WITH BUTTER AND CHEESE

You can make this fancier by the addition of any or all of the following: 2 tablespoons sauterne, 1/2 cup heavy cream, or 10 to 12 small mushrooms, sliced and sautéed in butter.

> 1 *lb. fettuccine (egg noodles)*
> 1/4 *lb. butter*

1/2 cup grated cheese—best quality parmesan or pecorino
1/2 tsp. fresh cracked black pepper

Boil the fettuccine *al dente*. While it is cooking melt the butter and heat the serving dish—a chafing dish or candle trivet is perfect here. Toss the drained fettuccine with 2 forks. When pasta is coated with butter, sprinkle in the cheese and pepper. Toss thoroughly and serve at once.

FETTUCCINE WITH PESTO

Like aglio-olio, this does not appeal to everyone. Like aglio-olio, it is likely to grow on you. Try a half a recipe at least once.

PESTO

6 cloves garlic
1/4 cup fresh basil leaves
  or 1/8 cup dried basil leaves
2 tbsp. parsley
1/2 tsp. salt
6 walnuts, shelled and chopped
1 cup olive oil
1/2 cup grated parmesan cheese

Combine all ingredients except cheese in the blender until smooth. Pour into bowl and stir in cheese. Let sit 3 or 4 hours at room temperature, or in the refrigerator overnight or longer.

To make pesto by hand: chop garlic, basil and parsley very fine on the chopping board. Then crush to a paste with salt and walnuts in the mortar. Transfer to a bowl and stir in the olive oil thoroughly, and then add the cheese.

This yields about 2 cups. One to 1-1/2 cups will dress 1 lb. linguine. Refrigerate any leftover pesto and use it as a dressing for raw or broiled tomatoes, or add it to tomato soup.

Add pesto to minestrone and it becomes minestrone genovese.

SWEDISH MACARONI

This is nice for a change once in a while. The celery gives it a brisk taste not usually associated with pasta dishes.

> 1/2 lb. elbow macaroni
> 8 strips bacon
> 1 small, tender stalk celery
> 2 medium onions
> 1 can tomato soup
>   or 1/2 pint canned tomatoes, thickened with 1 tsp. cornstarch and sweetened with 1 tsp. sugar
> 3 sprigs parsley, chopped
> salt and pepper to taste

Cook macaroni in salted water. Dice bacon and fry till crisp. Remove bacon with slotted spoon and pour most of the fat into the drippings can. Put the bacon on a small plate—if you cook it along with the vegetables it is sure to begin to burn. Sauté celery and onions in the bacon fat remaining in the pan until they soften. Add the soup or tomatoes, the crisp bacon, the parsley and the cooked, drained macaroni. Mix well, salt and pepper to taste, and turn into a casserole. Cover and bake at 300° for 45 minutes.

BAKED LASAGNE

On the few days of the year that I go to the city I make it a point to stop at the Italian market on S. 9th Street. One of these days the city planners will no doubt move it to standardize, modernize and sanitize. But meanwhile there are olives in variety in barrels, cheeses, and a good selection of fresh fruits and vegetables. And there is still at least one establishment where mozzarella and ricotta cheese are made from scratch for immediate consumption.

Supermarket mozzarella is tasteless and seems largely to turn to water when cooked; the ricotta smacks of a chemical reminiscent of your high school science days. But on 9th Street one can still get real cheese for lasagne. Once I get the cheese home, it takes less than an hour to get a pan of lasagne into the oven. The tomato gravy is either simmering on a back burner or in the refrigerator ready to use. If times are flush, there will even be meatballs (p. 134). Lasagna noodles are in a lard tin in the pantry. It is only a question of putting things together. If you have no tomato gravy, put the cheese in the refrigerator and make gravy (p. 31) today for tomorrow's lasagne.

Heat the tomato gravy and put a kettle of water on to boil. If there are no meatballs in your gravy and if you have ground beef on hand, you can make a skillet full of meatballs while the water for the pasta is heating.

Salt the water when it boils and add lasagna noodles. Half a pound of pasta is enough for 2 casseroles of lasagne. While the pasta is cooking, preheat the oven to 350°, slice the mozzarella and oil the inside of the casseroles or baking dishes.

Drain the cooked lasagne and separate at once, or the noodles may begin to stick together by the time you use the last of them.

Arrange a layer of noodles on the bottom of the casserole; top with a layer of mozzarella slices and slabs of ricotta. Ladle some gravy over the cheese. Repeat this process once. If you use casseroles which are 2 inches deep, 2 layers each of noodles, cheese and gravy will leave enough room for juices to bubble up without boiling over. Finish up with a layer of cheese and sauce. Do not leave meatballs on top or they will dry out too much in baking. Tuck them under a slab of cheese or push them down in a corner of the dish.

Bake lasagne about 25 minutes at 350°, or until the gravy is bubbling on top and the cheeses have melted.

Lasagne and a salad comprise a complete meal. Cool the second casserole and freeze.

CORNMEAL GNOCCHI

These are marvelous in winter—either as a first course alone, or to accompany veal or chicken.

> 3 cups milk
> 1 tsp. salt
> dash ground black pepper
> 1/4 tsp. nutmeg
> 3/4 cup yellow cornmeal
> 2 eggs
> 1-1/4 cups grated cheese
> 4 tbsp. butter

Bring milk, salt, pepper and nutmeg to boil in a heavy pan. Add the cornmeal slowly and steadily, stirring constantly. Cook and stir until the mixture thickens—the traditional rule of thumb is that *polenta* is done when a wooden spoon can stand up by itself in the center of the cornmeal. Remove from heat.

Beat the eggs and stir into them 1 cup of the grated cheese. Stir this mixture into the polenta. Spread the mixture on a greased baking sheet or large platter. Let sit for 2 or 3 hours, or refrigerate for 1 hour, to become firm. Cut the cornmeal in squares, triangles or circles and arrange in a single layer in a shallow baking dish. Melt the butter and drizzle it over the gnocchi, then sprinkle with remaining cheese. Bake at 400° for 15 minutes. Serve with a gravy boat of hot puréed tomato gravy.

BAKED MACARONI AND CHEESE

I'm very fond of macaroni and cheese but never want it to be so thin or so obviously economical that it reminds me of school cafeterias and summer camps. Three kinds of cheese and cream make this dish rich enough to serve as the entrée for a meatless meal.

1/2 cup cottage cheese or ricotta
1 package cream cheese (6 oz.)
1 cup light cream
  or 1 cup sour cream for extra-rich sauce
salt
2 cups elbow macaroni
3 pimientos chopped coarsely, optional
  or 3 tomatoes, canned or fresh, peeled and seeded, and
  chopped (also optional)
1 cup mild cheddar cheese, grated
  or 1/2 cup parmesan cheese, grated
2 tbsp. butter

Whip or blend cottage cheese and cream cheese together. Combine with cream and salt to taste. Boil macaroni *al dente,* drain very well and mix with the cheese-cream sauce. Add pimientos or tomatoes and pour into an oiled 2-quart casserole, sprinkling in the cheddar or parmesan cheese as you go. Reserve 1/4 cup of grated cheese. Dot the top of the pasta with the butter; sprinkle the 1/4 cup of cheese on top, and bake at 350° for 30 minutes.

HOMEMADE VEGETABLE NOODLE SOUP

When supplies are low and a trip to the store doesn't appeal for one reason or another, you can nearly always make a pot of vegetable soup with what is on hand. If you have a meaty soupbone in the refrigerator or freezer, so much the better, but you can make do without it by strengthening the stock with canned consommé or as many beef cubes as you can spare for what is meant to be a money-saving main dish. This recipe makes about 3 quarts.

1 cup white beans (pea, marrow, etc.), washed
meaty beef soupbone
1/4 cup barley
1/4 cup lentils
2 medium onions, diced
1 pt. tomatoes, coarsely chopped
2 medium carrots, diced
2 stalks celery, diced
1/2 pt. peas
1/2 pt. corn
3 sprigs parsley, chopped
1/2 tsp. thyme
1/4 tsp. celery seed
1 good-size bay leaf
1 cup noodles (elbows, ditalini, any small noodle)
salt and pepper to taste

Soak the beans for one hour in cold water so they will not take up much of the water for the soup stock. Bring the soaked beans to a boil in 2 quarts water (do not salt). Let beans boil 3 minutes. Reduce heat. Add soupbone, barley and lentils; cover pot and let simmer 20 minutes. Add all remaining ingredients except noodles and let simmer 1-1/2 hours, skimming occasionally. In a separate pan, cook noodles *al dente*, drain and add to soup 10 minutes before serving.

NOODLES AND BEANS (Pasta e fagioli)

This is more of a stew than a soup. Either way, it is hearty, filling and warming. Fish out the marrow if it hasn't disintegrated by serving time, if your family will not eat it. Or chop marrow finely.

1 cup white beans (pea, marrow, etc.), washed
5-inch piece of beef marrow
1 medium onion

1 stalk celery, diced
1 clove garlic, diced (optional)
4 sprigs parsley, diced fine
1/4 tsp. rosemary leaves, crumbled
2 tbsp. olive oil
1 tbsp. flour
1 tbsp. tomato paste in 2 tbsp. warm water
1 cup pasta—ditalini

Bring beans to a boil in about 2 quarts of water and reduce heat; add marrow and simmer until beans are tender. In a small skillet sauté onion, celery, garlic, parsley and rosemary in the olive oil. Sprinkle flour over this mixture and stir over a low flame. Add the tomato paste–water mixture and simmer 5 minutes. Add this sauce to the beans in the soup pot and let simmer for 1-1/2 to 2 hours. Add the ditalini and cook 12 to 15 minutes. Remove from heat and let stand 20 minutes. Reheat to serve.

POTATO GNOCCHI

This pasta is generally not available in stores and is easy to make. I only make gnocchi on cold days and serve them at lunch to people who are going to work or who play hard all afternoon.

4 medium potatoes
2 egg yolks
3 cups flour, approximate
1 tsp. salt

Boil and peel potatoes. Whip them in the electric mixer or put them through a ricer. Mix in the egg yolks. Mix flour and salt together in a large bowl or on a cutting board. Gradually work the flour into the potatoes until a dough-like consistency is reached. Roll the dough into strips about the thickness of your little finger. Cut into 1-inch pieces. Let the gnocchi dry for 30 minutes; then boil in plenty of salted water for 12 minutes. Drain and serve with tomato gravy and grated parmesan cheese.

BOILED POT PIE

This is composed of flat heavy noodles, chicken stock and some meat. I grew up loving it and now find that the younger the initiate, the more apt he is to like it. Pot pie is substantial fare. Accompany it with bowls of pepper hash (p. 155) and pickled beets and a simple green salad. Dessert should be nothing richer than an apple.

If you want to stretch a stewing chicken over several meals, stew a pound or two of chicken backs, too, and use the meat from the backs along with that from the wings, back, neck and drumsticks of the stewer. Use the white meat next day for creamed chicken, salad or sandwiches.

If you have leftover cooked veal or pork, you can substitute either for the chicken meat in the pot pie.

> 1-1/2 tbsp. butter
> 2 cups flour
> 1/2 tsp. salt
> 2 eggs, beaten
> 3 tbsp. water
> 2 cups chicken stock
> cooked chicken, pork or veal

Cut the butter into the flour and salt. Mix in the eggs, then the water. Roll out the dough on a well-floured board and let it rest for 20 minutes. Cut the dough into squares. Bring the stock to a gentle boil and drop the pot pie dough squares into it. Cover the kettle tightly and simmer for 20 minutes without uncovering. A functioning, loaded pepper mill on the table is essential.

You can add thinly sliced onions and chopped parsley to

the stock and meat to fancy up the taste and appearance, but to hardline pot pie devotées such frippery is merely distracting.

WINTER KEEPERS

Winter keepers are the vegetables, apples and nuts that can be stored whole and raw in cellars, attics or underground. To use freezer space and electricity to store prepared potatoes, onions and apples is becoming increasingly uneconomical.

CABBAGE

Late cabbages (ballhead and flat Dutch varieties) are good winter keepers. Grow or buy them and hang them by their roots from the roof of a cold storage house, or bury them, roots and all, in trenches and cover with earth and straw

If you grow your own cabbages and they are not sprayed according to the rigorous schedules of the commercial growers, you might keep in mind a piece of advice given by André Simon for the preparation of cabbage. In the funniest line I ever encountered in a book on food, M. Simon directs that cabbage be cut in quarters and "each quarter torn apart with the hands to make sure that there is no form of active animal left" (*Concise Encyclopaedia of Gastronomy*). The inference seems to be that any moribund, or even comatose, forms of animal life are allowable.

Winter cabbages can be prepared in any of the ways described in the first chapter. The recipes that follow seem to me particularly suited to cold weather.

Remember that cabbage, both green and red, discolors if cooked in iron. Use stainless steel, porcelain, enamel or earthenware.

STEAMED CABBAGE

This form of cabbage seems to me to go especially well with baked short ribs. When just barely cooked through and still crisp, it brings a light fresh accent to a winter meal. Steam cabbage five minutes before dinner is to be served.

1/2 head or 1 small head (about 1 lb.) of late cabbage
salt to taste
vinegar to taste

Halve the cabbage and remove the core and heavy ribs as carefully as you can. Cut the cabbage into wedges. Steam them in a steamer or colander over 1 inch of boiling water, making sure that no water touches the cabbage. Start testing the cabbage after 5 minutes—if it is not tender yet, it soon will be. Remove from the heat at once, sprinkle lightly with salt and vinegar, and serve.

If you are dealing with people who think they don't like cooked cabbage, do not let them see the application of the vinegar. Just fix the cabbage in the kitchen, arrange the wedges nicely on a serving dish and insist that the cabbage hater try it. Most people seem never to have had cabbage that was not grossly overcooked.

RED CABBAGE WITH APPLES

The sweet-sour quality of this dish and the tartness of the apples make it a perfect accompaniment for roast pork.

3 tbsp. butter
4 cups (about 1 lb.) shredded red cabbage, core and ribs removed
2 apples, preferably a tart cooking type, cored, pared and thinly sliced
1 tsp. salt
2 tbsp. brown sugar
1/2 cup water
3 tbsp. vinegar, approximate

Melt the butter in a saucepan that has a tight-fitting lid. Tilt the pan to be sure the sides are coated. Sauté the cabbage and apples for 3 minutes, turning gently with a wooden spoon. Sprinkle the salt and brown sugar over the cabbage, add the water and vinegar, and reduce heat. Cover and simmer until the cabbage is tender—usually from 10 to 15 minutes—stirring occasionally. Taste and add more vinegar if necessary.

RED CABBAGE SALAD

1 small head red cabbage
salt and pepper to taste
1/2 tsp. crushed coriander seeds
2 tbsp. vinegar
1 apple, peeled, cored and chopped
1 small onion, minced
3 tbsp. olive oil

Core the cabbage, remove heavy ribs and slice thinly or shred. Cover cabbage with boiling water and let sit 5 minutes. Drain well and put the cabbage in a salad bowl. Salt and pepper to taste, add remaining ingredients and toss well. Chill for at least 30 minutes and serve.

MARGARET'S PINK SAUERKRAUT

My dearest friend originated, so far as either of us knows, this treatment of sauerkraut. She used to serve it as a hot vegetable dish to accompany duck or pork, but refrigerator raiders thought it was even better cold, so she now serves it either way. Fresh cured sauerkraut which is usually sold in packs instead of cans is best for this dish.

2 packages fresh cured sauerkraut (2 lbs.)
3 tbsp. strained fat from good bacon
1/2 bottle "hot" ketchup
2 tbsp. sugar, approximate

Drain the juice from the sauerkraut—into a jar or glass if someone in the house likes to drink it. Put the kraut in a colander and run cold water through it for a few seconds. Let the kraut drain while you heat a heavy 3- or 4-quart saucepan. Melt the bacon fat, and add the kraut and enough water so that kraut is well covered, or, as Margaret says, "Enough water that it looks like a swamp there." Stir the kraut and keep an eye on it so that it doesn't boil over. Let it boil for a minute or two, then reduce heat and add the ketchup. Let the kraut simmer, partially covered, about 2-1/2 hours—until it is tender and most of the water has disappeared. Stir in 2 tbsp. sugar, taste, and add more if necessary. Do not add sugar earlier because it increases greatly the tendency of the kraut to burn. This is good reheated; add more water and watch and stir to avoid burning.

STOVE-TOP SAUERKRAUT WITH PORK

On gray winter mornings when it "felt like snow," my mother would say, "This is a good day for sauerkraut." The aroma of the kraut would tantalize me from after school to dinnertime. Now, years later, I still associate sauerkraut with a certain kind of day and wouldn't think of making it on a cloudless sunny day.

Use a pork shoulder, or frankfurters, or pig's feet, or, if the budget can stand it, all three.

> 3 lbs. sauerkraut
> water
> pork shoulder, about 3 lbs.
> 1 medium onion, sliced
> 2 apples, cored, peeled and quartered
> 1/2 tsp. caraway seed or juniper berries
> 4 pig's feet, scrubbed
> 8 frankfurters

If you like a mild-flavored kraut, drain it and squeeze out as much juice as you can. I like sour sauerkraut so I dump kraut, juice and all, in the pot. Put the kraut in a 10- or 12-quart soup pot, adding enough water to cover well. Put the pork shoulder in the kraut, and add the onion, apples and caraway or juniper berries. Cover loosely and cook over a medium-low heat for 3 hours. Bring the pork shoulder to the surface and remove bones, fat and gristle. Push the pork down into the kraut again. If you are having pig's feet, lay them now on top of the kraut. Cover and cook for 1 hour more. Add frankfurters to the pot 20 minutes before dinnertime. Serve with a big bowl of mashed potatoes. This combination is a complete meal.

CARROTS

Too often we think of cooked carrots as being either creamed or boiled and buttered, but cooked carrots can be an interesting change-of-pace vegetable. They also have a place on the relish tray, in the soup and salad bowls. I have tasted delicious carrot cakes in Berks and Lehigh counties in Pennsylvania but never have been able to obtain a recipe.

Raw carrots, scrubbed, scraped and cut in slender sticks, are good as a fresh salad. When lettuce is in short supply, arrange a centerpiece relish tray instead of a green salad. Pick four or five of the following for a colorful, easy-to-fix salad substitute: carrot sticks, celery, fennel, cucumber spears, strips of green pepper, olives, sour dill tomatoes (p. 150), pickled watermelon rind (p. 147), deviled eggs (p. 111), beet-pickled eggs (p. 112).

CARROT-CABBAGE SALAD

This has great appeal in mid-winter, when lettuce prices climb and there is home-grown cabbage in the cold house and carrots in sand in the cellar.

3 carrots
1/2 small head of cabbage (about 1/2 lb.)
2 tbsp. sugar
3 tbsp. vinegar
1/4 tsp. salt
pinch celery seed

Scrub and trim the carrots. Shred them on the coarse side of the grater. Remove the heavy ribs from the cabbage and shred or slice very thin. Dissolve the sugar in the vinegar. Combine the carrot and cabbage in a bowl, add the dressing, salt and celery seed, and toss well.

MARINATED CARROT SALAD

1/2 cup water
1/4 cup dry white wine
3 tbsp. salad oil
1 clove garlic, crushed
1 tsp. sugar
1/4 tsp. salt
1 bay leaf
1/4 tsp. celery seed
8 carrots

Combine all ingredients except carrots in a saucepan; bring to a boil, then simmer 5 minutes. Scrape the carrots and cut into strips. Boil them gently in water until they are just tender. Drain the carrots and put them at once in the marinade, and let cool. Arrange the carrots in a serving dish. Strain the marinade and use it to moisten the carrots. Chill well and serve.

CARROT PURÉE

This is an unusual soup—rich and sweet although it contains no sugar.

8 *carrots*
salt
water
2 *tbsp. butter*
pinch of nutmeg
1 *cup light cream*

Scrub and trim the carrots. Cut them in chunks and boil them in salted water until they just begin to soften. Drain. Purée the carrots in the blender or put them through the food mill. Pour the purée into a saucepan or in the top part of a double boiler over water—this last especially if you cannot keep an eye on the purée every minute. Stir in the butter and nutmeg. Gradually stir in the cream. Heat thoroughly but do not allow to boil.

SOUR CREAMED CARROTS

8 *carrots*
2 *tbsp. butter*
1 *cup sour cream*
salt to taste

Scrub and trim carrots and cut into 1/4-inch-thick rounds. Melt the butter in a skillet and sauté the carrots until they are tender. Add the sour cream and salt to taste. Stir and heat through but do not allow to boil.

COMPANY CARROTS

10 carrots, scrubbed and trimmed
3 tbsp. butter
1 tsp. confectioners sugar
1 tbsp. vodka
   or 1 tbsp. orange liqueur
1/2 cup water
1/2 cup seedless grapes
salt to taste
dash tabasco sauce (optional)

Cut carrots in rounds and sauté in the butter about 5 minutes. Dust the carrots with the confectioners sugar and let cook 1 or 2 minutes longer, stirring meanwhile so they do not stick. Add the vodka or orange liqueur and water, stirring now until the butter and sugar combine with the fluid to make a sauce. Add grapes and simmer, covered, until carrots are quite tender. Salt to taste and add tabasco if you like. Black pepper— either ground or cracked—does mar the appearance of the carrots and grapes.

CANDIED CARROTS

8   carrots, scrubbed, trimmed and cut in strips
2 cups water
1 tsp. salt
2 tbsp. sugar
3 tbsp. butter

Put all ingredients in a saucepan; stir and bring to a boil. Reduce the heat, cover the pan and simmer until liquid is reduced to a syrup. Serve carrots with syrup spooned over them.

Vary this by substituting maple syrup for the sugar and adding 1 tsp. vinegar.

ONIONS

We tend to think of onions as a seasoning or relish except for their occasional appearance as a creamed vegetable. These two dishes use onions as a main ingredient and are a little different.

BAKED ONIONS

4 *large onions*
butter
2 *tbsp. brown sugar*
salt
1 *tsp. lemon juice*
1/4 *tsp. paprika*
3 *sprigs parsley, finely chopped*

Skin and halve onions and arrange in a shallow, well buttered baking dish. Sprinkle with brown sugar, salt lightly and dot with butter. Bake at 350° until onions are tender—which will depend upon the size and type of onion. Sprinkle with lemon juice, paprika and chopped parsley.

APPLES, ONIONS AND RAISINS

This goes well with any pork dish.

2 *tbsp. bacon fat*
4 *medium onions, peeled and quartered*
4 *apples, cored and quartered*
1/4 *cup raisins, soaked in water to plump*
salt to taste

Melt the bacon fat in a skillet and sauté onions and apples until they begin to soften. Add raisins; cover and simmer about 10 minutes. Salt to taste—bacon fat will supply some saltiness.

ACORN SQUASH

BAKED ACORN SQUASH

2 *acorn squash (1/2 for each person)*
2 *tbsp. butter*
1/2 *jigger rum*
2 *tbsp. cream*
1 *tbsp. brown sugar*
1/4 *tsp. nutmeg*
salt and pepper to taste
butter

Cut squash in half, remove fibers and seeds, and bake face down on a baking dish at 350° until the meat of the squash is tender (about 30 to 45 minutes). Scoop out meat, being careful not to pierce the skin, since the shells must be used. Beat the squash smooth, adding to it the butter, rum, cream, brown sugar and nutmeg. Salt and pepper to taste. Spoon the mixture into the shells and place, cut side up, in the baking dish. Use props of crumpled aluminum foil to keep them upright. Dot the surface with butter, reheat in 350° oven, and serve.

POTATOES

Almost every cookbook gives a variety of potato recipes, to which I have little to add. One gets tired of mashed, boiled and French fried potatoes. Vary mashed potatoes from time to time by whipping in sour cream instead of milk, or stir grated cheddar cheese into mashed potatoes, turn them into a baking dish, dot with butter and bake at 350° until they begin to brown on top.

When new red potatoes are plentiful, take advantage of the season. Boil them and serve them in their jackets. Serve with butter and salt. Their waxy texture and tasty skins are a pleasant change from the more familiar brown-skinned potatoes.

SPICY SCALLOPED POTATOES

Bake a casserole of these along with a meat loaf.

> 4 *medium to large potatoes*
> *salt*
> *flour*
> *quatre épices (p. 167)*
> *1/2 cup grated cheddar or gruyère cheese*
> *butter*
> *milk*

Pare and slice potatoes. Put a layer of potatoes in a baking dish. Sprinkle the layer with salt, flour, quatre épices and cheese. Dot with butter. Repeat this process until all potatoes have been used. Add milk until you can see it around the edges of the topmost potatoes. Cover the dish and bake at 300° until the potatoes are soft. It is wise to put a cookie sheet or a piece of aluminum foil under the dish in the oven since, if you put a little too much milk, it may boil over and make a mess. When potatoes are tender, remove the cover and let the top brown for about 15 minutes.

APPLES

Like asparagus and tomatoes, apples are economical to buy in comparatively large amounts—by the basket—at roadside stands and farmers' markets. If you have a cold cellar or can store apples underground, you can keep them as they come from the basket until needed. If you have no storage facilities, put a dozen apples in the refrigerator for salads and eating out of hand, and convert the rest to applesauce (p. 95), pie filling, jelly (p. 168) and chutney (p. 161). See page 175 for directions for drying apples.

FRIED APPLES

These are so good and so easy to make that it is hard to understand why more people don't make them. Many of my guests claim to have never tasted them before. Fried apples go well with sausage, ham and roast pork.

> *bacon fat or butter*
> *4 apples*
> *light brown sugar*

Melt bacon fat or butter in a large skillet or on the grill. Core and slice apples but do not pare. Fry apple slices gently about 5 minutes. Turn them and sprinkle the fried side with the sugar. Let cook another 5 minutes—until the sugar melts and is absorbed in the apple. Remove as done to a heated platter and keep in the oven until ready to serve.

A slightly fancier version: Coat apple slices with lightly salted flour and fry. Simmer a sauce of 1 tbsp. melted butter, 1/4 cup white wine, 1 tsp. sugar and a pinch of cinnamon. Drizzle the sauce over the apples just before serving.

APPLE CRISP

I like this and Brown Betty because they can bake during the last half hour with just about whatever is in the oven. Both these country desserts are faster and easier to put together than a pie, and all the ingredients are always on hand.

> *6 apples, pared, cored and sliced thin*
> *1 tbsp. lemon juice*
> *1 cup uncooked oatmeal*
> *1/3 cup flour*
> *3/4 cup brown sugar, packed firmly*
> *1/2 tsp. salt*
> *1/2 tsp. cinnamon*
> *1/8 tsp. ground clove*
> *1/3 cup melted butter*

Put apple slices in a buttered baking dish and sprinkle with lemon juice. Combine all remaining ingredients, mix well and spread mixture over the apples. Bake at 375° 30 minutes. Serve while still warm.

This is good in summer, made with peaches instead of apples.

BROWN BETTY

4 cups apples, cored, pared and sliced thin
2 cups bread, cut in bite-size pieces
1 cup brown sugar
cinnamon
butter
1/3 cup hot water

Arrange a layer of apple slices in a buttered baking dish or loaf pan. Add a layer of bread, sprinkle with sugar and cinnamon, and dot with butter. Repeat. You should have enough apples left to make a top layer of apples. Sprinkle with remaining sugar and cinnamon. Pour the hot water over the Brown Betty and bake at 350° for 30 to 40 minutes. Serve hot or cold with cream.

APPLESAUCE

This recipe produces a sauce of more robust texture and color than the pale sauce that comes from the store and which always reminds me of hospital trays. This recipe makes about one quart, but you can use as many apples as you want or have on hand. Sauce will keep well in the refrigerator for one week.

10 to 12 apples, cored but not peeled
sugar
cinnamon

Cut the apples in quarters and stew them in just enough water to cover until they are quite soft. Put the apples in the potato ricer and force out as much pulp as you can. Add sugar and cinnamon to taste.

To can apple sauce: Ladle the hot sauce into sterilized jars to 1/4 inch from the top; seal and process in a hot water bath for 10 minutes.

To can apples, pare, core and slice apples into 2 quarts of water to which 1 tbsp. salt and 1 tbsp. vinegar has been added. This will help to prevent discoloring. When all apples have been sliced, drain and cook them in a syrup of 3 cups water and 1 cup sugar. Pack the apples in jars; cover with the hot syrup to 1/2 inch from the top, and seal. Process in boiling water for 15 minutes.

Approximately 7 cups sliced apples yield 1 quart canned apples.

CHAPTER 4

Eggs,
Poultry and
Inexpensive Meat Dishes

EGGS

I HAVE a constant supply of eggs. Since my hens are money makers, the eggs I use are, in a sense, free. I eat eggs for breakfast, lunch and dinner, and in desserts, drinks and snacks. With a functioning henhouse and well-stocked pantry I can always put together a company meal—on very short notice if need be.

If you have hens, you will soon learn that they don't all lay their eggs in the nesting boxes every day. The eggs you find in the runs and the corners of the henhouse can be checked for freshness by putting them in heavily salted water (12%). Fresh eggs will go to the bottom and stay there. Discard bobbers and floaters. Eggs lose a little weight each day. If you pick up an egg that is amazingly light, don't waste the salt. Just carry the egg carefully to the compost heap. I feed cracked and checked eggs to the dogs.

I keep a small basket of eggs on a kitchen counter. I never refrigerate the eggs I know I am going to use. Breakfast eggs, a salad dressing for lunch, a batch of cup custards and a platter of deviled eggs will require the use of 18 eggs by noontime.

Keep the day's supply of eggs at room temperature: they are less apt to crack in hot water, the yolks and whites mix more easily and the whites beat to a greater volume.

The following are my favorite ways of preparing eggs. All these recipes are easy, quick and inexpensive. From time to time try some of the fancier variations on standard egg dishes to be found in books on French cooking. The *Larousse gastronomique* (New York: Crown, 1961) devotes 27 pages to eggs, *The Escoffier Cook Book* (New York: Crown, 1964), 31 pages. Some will become favorites.

Eggs for breakfast are common enough. I offer no recipes for breakfast eggs, only two suggestions.

Fry eggs gently. Fried eggs are too often cooked over too high a flame—the edges of the white are brown and rubbery and sometimes must be cut with a *knife!* Fry eggs over a steady, moderate heat in a shallow frying pan whose cooking surface has always been well treated. Melt enough butter to coat the pan. The butter should melt quietly—if it sizzles, the pan is too hot. Break the eggs gently into the pan, salt them lightly and cook until the whites are firm and have lost all transparency. Covering the pan will let the eggs fry more quickly but the yolks may become a little cloudy looking. Dust the eggs with freshly ground black pepper and slide them onto a heated plate. Beautiful, bright and tender, gently fried eggs will appeal even to those who think they don't like fried eggs.

Scrambled eggs are practically foolproof when cooked in the top part of a double boiler. Many cookbooks give this advice but like so much good advice, it seems to be seldom heeded. While the eggs cook slowly over hot water, you need only give them a stir or two while attending to the bacon and toast. The eggs will stay creamy and soft and hot much longer than when cooked over direct heat.

If you have some leftover mushrooms, chicken livers, paté or cheese, use them to dress up scrambled eggs for lunch. Add 1 tbsp. of leftovers, finely chopped, for every two eggs and let them cook together. For additional richness, add a dash of cream—1/4 cup for every two eggs. While the eggs are scrambling, you have time to make a green salad and heat some rolls. This is a hearty, attractive lunch that can be got together in 10 minutes and is a good deal more satisfying than sandwiches and a cup of instant soup.

MAYONNAISE

This sauce that most of us use in some way every day has lately become quite expensive. Make your own—especially if you have an abundance of eggs. Homemade mayonnaise is tastier and more nutritious than commercial preparations and about one third as expensive.

> 2 *egg yolks*
> 1 *tsp. dry mustard*
> 1/2 *tsp. salt*
> 4 *tbsp. vinegar*
> 2 *cups olive oil or blended salad oil*

Have all ingredients at room temperature. Beat the egg yolks until pale yellow. Mix the mustard and salt thoroughly, making sure all lumps are pressed out of the mustard. Add mixture and half of the vinegar to the egg yolks. Mix thoroughly. Add oil drop by drop while beating steadily. As the oil blends more readily, pour it in steadily and slowly while continuing to beat the mayonnaise. Add the remaining 2 tbsp. vinegar and stop beating the minute it has been completely mixed in.

Yield: 2-1/4 cups.

BLENDER MAYONNAISE

1 egg
1 cup salad oil
juice of 1 lemon
1/4 tsp. dry mustard
1/4 tsp. salt

Put egg, 1/4 cup oil (more or less), lemon juice, mustard and salt in blender. Cover and blend a few seconds on low speed. Remove cover and add remaining oil in a slow, steady stream. Turn off blender the minute the last of the oil is incorporated.

Yield: 1-1/4 cups.

EGG AND ONION SANDWICHES

This simple and unsubtle sandwich is a summer favorite at my house when the greenery is either lettuce from the garden or watercress. Spread French, Italian or homemade white bread with mayonnaise. Fill the sandwich with a layer of thinly sliced hardboiled egg, a layer of *very* thinly sliced onion and a generous layer of lettuce or watercress. Allow one egg for each sandwich.

EGG SALAD SANDWICHES

4 hardboiled eggs, chopped
1 tbsp. green pepper, chopped
1 tbsp. celery, chopped
1 tsp. onion, chopped
salt to taste
dash tabasco sauce
mayonnaise to bind

Combine all ingredients and mix well. If there is no green pepper, substitute 1 tbsp. chopped sweet pickle.

Spread the egg salad on warm toast or just-sliced French or Italian bread. Add a layer of crisp lettuce. Serve these sandwiches with a substantial soup in winter, or with a light cold soup in summer, for a complete and tasty lunch. Serves 4.

EGG MAIN DISHES

These three dishes are easy to prepare and require no exotic ingredients. They can be put together in minutes with what's on hand, and are attractive, nutritious and very economical.

CREOLE EGGS IN A SKILLET

1 small onion, finely chopped
1 small green pepper, seeded and diced
1 tbsp. vegetable oil
8 oz. tomato sauce (half-pint jar of home-canned sauce)
1 4-oz. can mushrooms, if you have them
1/8 tsp. thyme
salt, pepper and sherry to taste
4 eggs

Cook onion and green pepper in oil over medium heat about 3 minutes. Add the tomato sauce, mushrooms and their liquid and the seasonings. Reduce heat. Stir and simmer until well blended. Add the raw eggs one at a time, taking care that they remain whole. Cover and let simmer about 10 minutes or until the whites are set. Serve on rice, egg noodles, muffin halves or, failing all else, toast. Serves 2.

EGG LOAF

12 hardboiled eggs, peeled
1/4 lb. butter, soft
1/4 cup celery, finely diced
1/4 cup green olives, diced
generous dash of tabasco sauce
salt and pepper to taste

Put the eggs and butter in a bowl and cut them together with 2 knives or a pastry blender. Add the celery, olives and seasonings to the mixture and blend thoroughly. Pack the mixture in a loaf pan lined with wax paper and chill about 3 hours. Serve slices on a bed of lettuce.

To make a spread for hors d'oeuvres, substitute black olives and capers for the green olives and celery.

EGGS AURORE

6 hardboiled eggs
2 tbsp. soft butter
3 tbsp. tomato purée or sauce
1/2 tsp. salt
pinch black pepper
2 tbsp. butter
2 tbsp. flour
1 cup milk
salt and pepper to taste
1/2 cup tomato purée

Cut the eggs in half lengthwise and scoop yolks into a small bowl. Mash the yolks and combine well with 2 tbsp. butter, 3 tbsp. tomato purée, 1/2 tsp. salt and dash of pepper. Stuff the egg whites with this mixture and arrange them in a shallow buttered casserole. Heat the eggs in a 300° oven but don't let them brown.

Make a white sauce of the butter, flour and milk, seasoning to taste. Combine the mixture with the 1/2 cup tomato purée and coat the eggs with this "aurore" sauce. Garnish with chopped hardboiled egg yolk, parsley or chervil.

To make a fancy dish, decorate the eggs and border the casserole with mashed potatoes forced through a pastry bag. Serve the remaining sauce in a gravy boat.

EGG DESSERTS

Here are eight desserts that depend on eggs. They range from light and gooey, like versatile custard, to heavy and gooey, like Texas Dessert—one small portion of which is guaranteed to spoil any appetite for at least three hours.

CUSTARD

I like this recipe because it contains no flour, which makes it foolproof and reduces to practically never a need to strain the custard to remove lumps.

> 6 *egg yolks* or 4 *whole eggs*
> 2 *cups scalded milk*
> 1/4 *cup sugar (perhaps a little more)*
> 1/8 *tsp. salt*
> 1/2 *tsp. vanilla*

In the top part of a double boiler, beat the egg yolks until they are creamy and pale yellow. Scald milk by heating until a skin forms on top. Do not turn your back when milk is on the stove; it can boil over in seconds and is a dreadful mess to clean up. Add the sugar, salt and milk to the egg yolks. Cook over simmering, never boiling, water until the mixture coats the spoon and holds—that is, the coating on the spoon stays on evenly and does not drip off. Remove the custard from the heat, stir in the vanilla and let cool.

Use custard as a sauce over sliced peaches or any berries. Flavor custard with a dash of sherry or rum or a drop of almond extract, and spoon it over pound cake that is past its prime.

FLOATING ISLAND

Use custard to make this old-fashioned dessert, now so seldom served it has become a novelty. Pour custard into a shallow ovenproof baking dish. In a mixing bowl, add 1/4 tsp. salt to 6 egg whites and beat until the whites form peaks. Beat in 5 tbsp. sugar and 1 tsp. vanilla. Dot the custard with spoonfuls of the meringue mixture. Bake in a hot (500°) oven until the meringue peaks begin to brown—usually between 4 and 6 minutes.

CUP CUSTARDS

In my house cup custards serve more as mid-morning or late evening snacks than as dessert. My mother used to have them, already chilled, ready for an after-school snack. Make them every once in a while—especially when young appetites need to be calmed until meal time.

> 3 *eggs*
> 1/2 *cup sugar, heaping*
> 1/8 *tsp. salt*
> 1 *tsp. vanilla*
> 1 *qt. milk, scalded*
> *nutmeg to taste*

In a large bowl, beat the eggs; add the sugar, salt and vanilla. Pour the scalded milk into the mixture and stir well to make sure that sugar is dissolved. Pour into custard cups or any baking dish and sprinkle with freshly grated nutmeg. Put the cups in a pan of hot water and bake at 300° until a knife stuck in the middle comes out clean.

Yield: 8 eight-ounce custard cups.

CORNSTARCH PUDDING *(also known as vanilla pudding)*

2 *tbsp. butter*
1/4 *cup cornstarch*
1/2 *cup sugar*
1/2 *tsp. salt.*
2 *cups milk*
2 *egg yolks, beaten*
1 *tsp. vanilla*

Melt the butter. Mix the cornstarch, sugar and salt, and blend with the butter. Add the milk gradually and bring to a boil, stirring constantly. Pour a small amount of this mixture into the egg yolks and mix. Then add remainder and mix well. Cook over low heat for 2 or 3 minutes. Cover and let cool. Add vanilla. If the pudding is too thick, beat in enough cream to produce the consistency you want.

CHOCOLATE PUDDING

This can be served in individual bowls just as it is. My favorite use of chocolate pudding is in the concoction of a dessert that is somewhat lacking in sophistication but very satisfying. Put a slab of pound cake in the bottom of a soup bowl and spread the cake with slightly softened vanilla ice cream. Spoon chocolate pudding over ice cream, whipped cream over the pudding, and top with a maraschino cherry.

2-1/2 *oz. (2-1/2 squares) chocolate*
2/3 *cup sugar*
3 *cups milk*
1/4 *tsp. salt*
5 *egg yolks*
1/2 *tsp. vanilla*

Melt chocolate in the top part of a double boiler, over hot water. Add the sugar and milk and combine well with the chocolate. Remove from the heat; add salt and gradually stir into the egg yolks. Return the mixture to the double boiler and cook over simmering water until the pudding thickens. Remove from the heat, stir in vanilla, and pour the pudding into custard cups, sherbet glasses or one large serving dish.

TEXAS DESSERT

This recipe comes from the cafeteria of the Federal Reserve Bank of Dallas, Texas. There it was taken more or less for granted. Dieters avoided it, of course. It has been a great success here in south Jersey. The first time it appears everyone will ask what the ingredients are. Don't tell them.

> *4 tbsp. melted butter*
> *1/2 lb. gingersnaps*
> *2-1/2 cups confectioners sugar*
> *1/4 lb. soft butter*
> *3 eggs*
> *3 small bananas*
> *1 no. 2 can diced pineapple, drained*
> *3/4 cup pecans*
> *1 cup whipping cream, whipped*

Spread 4 tbsp. melted butter in a dish which is 9 by 14 inches or equivalent. Roll the gingersnaps into fine crumbs and spread evenly over the butter. Set in the refrigerator to chill. Cream the confectioners sugar and soft butter together; add whole eggs one at a time, creaming after each addition. Continue beating until the mixture becomes fluffy. Spread over the chilled crumbs and return to refrigerator. Dice the bananas and pineapple and combine with the pecans. Fold this mixture into the whipped cream. Spread over the sugar-butter layer and sprinkle with a few gingersnap crumbs. Chill

2 hours before serving. This recipe serves 10, but you will have some left over for next-day snacking, since it's practically impossible to get 10 people together who would all eat this dessert.

LEMON SPONGE PUDDING

This pudding separates as it bakes so that, when it is finished, the pudding is beneath a fluffy crust.

1 lemon
1 cup sugar
1/8 tsp. salt
2 tbsp. flour
2 egg yolks
1 cup milk
2 egg whites

Grate the rind of the lemon into a bowl. Add sugar, salt and flour and mix well. Add the juice of the lemon and the egg yolks. Mix thoroughly. Add the milk and stir until smooth. In a small bowl, beat the egg whites until very stiff. Fold the whites into the lemon mixture until the white completely disappears. Pour into a baking dish and put the dish in a pan of hot water. Bake at 300° (not one bit hotter) about one hour. When the top is lightly browned, the pudding is finished. Do not refrigerate until the pudding has cooled completely, or it may separate.

CHOCOLATE SOUFFLÉ

This is a fine dessert and easy. The most important point is to be sure that all diners are ready to eat it the minute it leaves the oven.

> 1/2 cup butter
> 1/4 cup flour
> 1/4 tsp. salt
> 2 oz. (2 squares) unsweetened chocolate
> 3/4 cup milk
> 3 egg yolks
> 1/2 cup sugar
> 3 egg whites
> 1/2 tsp. cream of tartar

Combine butter, flour, salt and chocolate in the top part of a double boiler. When butter and chocolate have melted completely and the mixture is perfectly smooth, stir in the milk gradually and cook over simmering water until the mixture thickens. Remove from heat.

In a small bowl, beat egg yolks until they are thick, then gradually beat in 1/2 cup sugar. Add a little of the chocolate mixture to the yolks, then pour the yolk mixture into the chocolate and blend well. Combine the egg whites and cream of tartar in a small bowl and beat until stiff. Fold the egg whites into the chocolate. Pour the mixture into a buttered 2-qt. soufflé dish or baking dish. Set in a pan of water and bake at 350° about 45 minutes, when the soufflé will be nicely puffed and brown. Serve hot accompanied by a bowl of chilled custard (p. 103) for those who like to gild the lily. This serves 4 people generously, 6 adequately.

COCONUT CREAM PIE

There are a number of people who believe that this is the same as Coconut Custard Pie. Coconut cream will not hold its shape when cut the way custard does but it is richer and, to my taste, more delicious. If you have the time, or a child or guest that you can put to work, grate your own fresh coconut.

2 *tbsp. butter*
1/3 *cup cornstarch*
1/2 *cup sugar*
1/2 *tsp. salt*
2 *cups milk*
2 *egg yolks, slightly beaten*
1 *8-oz. can coconut or fresh grated coconut*
1 *tsp. vanilla*
1/2 *cup whipping cream, whipped*

Melt butter. Over low heat blend in cornstarch, sugar and salt. If you are apprehensive about burning the mixture, use the top part of a large double boiler. Gradually add the milk, blending carefully, and increase the heat. When all the milk has been added, bring the mixture to a gentle boil and stir until the mixture thickens. Reduce the heat to very low and mix a little of the mixture with the egg yolks, then add yolks to the mixture. Let simmer over low heat 2 minutes. *Do not allow to boil.* Remove from heat and add most of the coconut; put aside 2 or 3 tbsp. of coconut. Stir the pie filling to distribute the coconut evenly, then let cool. Spread the reserved 2 tbsp. coconut in a pie pan and toast it in a 300° oven until it browns. Stir frequently and watch carefully—fresh coconut burns more quickly than canned.

When the filling has cooled, stir in vanilla and pour the mixture into a baked pie shell. Cover with whipped cream, sprinkle with toasted coconut and refrigerate until serving time.

SNACKS

I use eggs a good deal for snacks—between-meal pick-me-ups like milkshakes and deviled eggs. Pickled eggs and sardine paté usually first appear at lunch; the leftovers are good snack material—in sandwiches or out of hand.

Milkshakes are very simple to make. The basic ingredients are flavored syrup, ice cream, milk and eggs. For a chocolate milkshake for two people, put 4 tbsp. chocolate syrup, 2 eggs and chocolate ice cream to taste in the blender. Cover; blend a few seconds on low speed, then high. Add 1 quart milk, and blend on high speed 5 seconds to mix thoroughly. Serve. Strawberry syrup and strawberry ice cream make a good milkshake with eggs and milk.

Try a combination of vanilla syrup, 2 bananas, and a good dash of nutmeg or cinnamon with ice cream and milk. Eggnog milkshake is popular here. To 1 quart of milk add vanilla syrup to taste (I use 4 tbsp.), 4 eggs, vanilla ice cream to suit, a good pinch of nutmeg, 2 ounces of rum (more or less) and a dash of salt. Taste before you pour the milkshake from the blender and add more of any ingredient to suit your taste.

The simplest egg snack of all is a hardboiled egg eaten out of hand. A quartered egg on lettuce dressed with mayonnaise and capers is a quickly fixed light appetizer. Hardboiled eggs dressed with a *tapenade* sauce are something special: serve the peeled, halved or quartered eggs on a platter, and pass a bowl of sauce. Leftover sauce will keep well in the refrigerator for several days and is a good dressing for sliced tomatoes or salads.

TAPENADE

1/2 cup black olives, pitted and chopped
1 2-5/8-oz. can anchovies, drained
1 3-oz. can tuna fish, drained

1/2 tsp. dry mustard
3 tbsp. capers, drained
1/2 cup salad oil
3 tbsp. lemon juice
1-1/2 oz. brandy

Pound the first 5 ingredients to a smooth paste in a mortar. Gradually add the oil, then the juice and brandy. Mix well and let stand at least 3 hours before using. Store in a covered jar in the refrigerator.

DEVILED EGGS

12 eggs, hardboiled and shelled
1 tsp. dry mustard (more for additional zippiness)
1 tsp. parsley, very finely chopped
2 tsp. chives, very finely chopped
2 tsp. tarragon, very finely chopped
dash Worcestershire sauce
salt and pepper to taste
mayonnaise

Halve eggs lengthwise. Scoop yolks into a bowl; add all ingredients except mayonnaise and mash together, mixing thoroughly. Blend in mayonnaise until mixture is spreadable but still very firm. Stuff the egg whites neatly with the mixture, mounding slightly and smoothing the surface. Arrange the deviled eggs on lettuce. If you want to sprinkle a little paprika on each egg, make a small paper funnel to be sure none of the paprika gets on the white of the egg.

Every once in a while substitute finely crumbled crisp bacon for tarragon.

PLAIN PICKLED EGGS

Make a 10% saltwater brine and add a handful of yellow onion skins. Crack but do not shell 12 hardboiled eggs; put them in the brine and keep them submerged for at least 2 days prior to serving.

SPICED PICKLED EGGS

2/3 *cup vinegar*
1/3 *cup brown sugar*
4 *cups water*
3 *tbsp. tea leaves* or 2 *tea bags*
3 *tbsp. soy sauce*
3 *tsp. salt*
1 *tsp. fennel or anis seed*
12 *hardboiled eggs, shelled*

Combine vinegar, sugar and water in a saucepan and bring to a boil. Add tea and let steep 5 minutes. Strain or remove teabags. Add soy sauce, salt and spice. Put the eggs in the pickling liquid and simmer very gently 1 hour. Let cool. Put the eggs, still in their liquid, into a wide-mouth jar; cover and refrigerate 3 days before serving.

BEET-PICKLED EGGS

These colorful pickled eggs are traditional Pennsylvania Dutch fare.

10 *small beets or the equivalent of larger beets*
1/4 *cup brown sugar*
1/2 *cup vinegar*
1/2 *cup cold water*
1 *inch-long stick cinnamon*
4 *cloves*
12 *hardboiled eggs, shelled*

Boil the beets until tender. Slip off the skins. Combine the remaining ingredients except eggs in a saucepan; add the beets and boil gently for 10 minutes. Let cool and refrigerate for 2 days. Remove the beets and use as pickled beets. Add the eggs to the beet liquid, refrigerate, and let pickle for at least 2 days before serving.

SARDINE PÂTÉ

3 cans sardines, drained
6 hardboiled eggs, finely chopped
2 small onions, very finely chopped
1 tbsp. parsley, finely chopped
salt and pepper to taste
mayonnaise
1 tsp. brandy
lemon juice to taste

Blend sardines, eggs, onions, parsley, salt and pepper until mixture is smooth. Stir in mayonnaise until paté is bound. Add brandy and lemon juice. Pack in a serving dish and chill. Serve with toast rounds or crackers. Use any leftovers next day as a sandwich filling.

CHICKEN

The henhouse provides frying and broiling chicken in summer, stewing chicken year round. In June, July and August, I fry or barbecue the cockerels that hatched in April and May. Laying hens who are no longer earning their keep or who have acquired bad habits such as egg eating go into the pot to provide meat for soups, sandwiches, salads and main course dishes.

This schedule works well. The fryer-broilers are on hand in the outdoor cooking season. I like to do most frying, broiling and cornhusking outside because it prevents so much mess in the kitchen.

Sauces and marinades keep broiled and fried chicken from becoming monotonous. You can use leftover jams, jellies, relishes, baby-food fruit preparations, and fresh fruits and vegetables as bases for sweet-sour sauces. Simply add equal amounts of sugar, brown or white; or honey and vinegar, salt to taste; water to thin; and heat to blend. Add herbs, ketchup, soy sauce, etc., according to your mood. Here's a sample recipe for a sweet-sour sauce. You can substitute any tart fruit from apricots to lingonberries.

SWEET-SOUR SAUCE

> 1 tbsp. oil
> 1 tbsp. onion, finely diced
> 1 clove garlic, finely diced
> 1 cup peach preserves
> 1/4 cup brown sugar
> 1/4 cup vinegar
> dash Worcestershire sauce
> 1/2 tsp. salt

Heat a small saucepan, and put in oil, onion and garlic. Sauté a minute or two but don't let garlic and onion brown. Add remaining ingredients. Heat and stir until thoroughly mixed. Thicken with 1 tsp. cornstarch mixed with 2 tbsp. water if you want to use the sauce to glaze broiled chicken. Otherwise, serve the sauce in a gravy boat.

PARSLEY-ALMOND SAUCE

This sauce comes from Mexico, where it is known as *salsa de perejil y almendras*. Spread on broiled chicken or pork just before serving.

1 cup chopped parsley, tightly packed
1/4 cup almonds, blanched
3 tbsp. vinegar
6 tbsp. olive oil
1 tsp. salt

Cook parsley in 1 cup water until tender, and drain. Grind the parsley and almonds together in a mortar; add vinegar, oil and salt and blend well.

MARINADES

4 oz. bourbon
4 oz. peanut oil
4 oz. soy sauce
1 inch piece fresh ginger root, crushed
1 garlic clove, crushed

Combine all ingredients. Marinate raw chicken in the mixture for at least 6 hours. Drain chicken and broil, basting frequently with marinade.

2 tbsp. tarragon
3 sprigs parsley
1/2 tsp. dry oregano
2 tbsp. sugar
2 tsp. salt
1 tsp. cracked pepper
1 cup salad oil
1/4 cup wine vinegar
3 tbsp. ketchup

Combine all ingredients.

Marinate chicken in refrigerator, turning occasionally, for 24 hours. Broil over charcoal, basting frequently with the marinade. For the last basting, thicken the remaining marinade with cornstarch or arrowroot so that final bastings coat and glaze the chicken.

> *1/4 lb. butter*
> *1/4 tsp. tarragon*
> *1/2 tsp. marjoram*
> *1 cup dry white wine*
> *1/2 cup salad oil*
> *3 tbsp. soy sauce*
> *1 garlic clove, crushed*
> *1/2 tsp. salt*

Mix the butter, tarragon and marjoram and, using a narrow spatula or a dull knife, insert the butter mixture beneath the skin of the breast portion of halved broilers. Combine the wine, oil, soy sauce, garlic and salt and marinate the broiler halves in the mixture 4 or 5 hours, or better yet, overnight. Broil the halves, basting with the remaining marinade.

CHICKEN TARRAGON

> *3 tbsp. fresh tarragon leaves or 1 tbsp. dried leaves*
> *3/4 cup dry white wine*
> *1/8 lb. butter*
> *1 frying chicken, cut up*
> *1 tsp. salt*
> *pepper to taste*

Rub the tarrragon between your fingers to bruise or crumble and let it soak in the wine for one hour. Melt the butter in a large frying pan or Dutch oven and sear chicken quickly; season with salt and pepper. Reduce heat, cover pan and let chicken cook slowly for 20 minutes. Remove the cover; increase heat, and add wine and tarragon. Cook, stirring frequently and turning chicken, until the chicken is done and the sauce is reduced to 2 or 3 tbsp.

If you want to make a sauce to serve separately with the chicken or on rice, remove the chicken and keep it warm while you stir 1/2 cup chicken stock into the drippings. When the drippings are well mixed into the stock, add 1/2 cup cream. Reduce heat so that sauce does not boil. Thicken with 1 tsp. cornstarch in 3 tbsp. water and salt to taste.

GARLIC BAKED CHICKEN

1/8 lb. butter
1 frying chicken, cut up
salt and pepper
1 tsp. garlic powder
1/2 cup sliced fresh mushrooms or small can mushrooms

Melt the butter in a casserole large enough to accommodate the chicken. Coat each piece of chicken well with the butter; salt and pepper them and sprinkle with garlic powder. Bake the chicken, uncovered, at 450°. Turn each piece over after 15 minutes. When the chicken is nicely browned, pour the mushrooms over the chicken, turn off the oven and remove the casserole after 10 minutes.

BAKED CHICKEN IN YOGURT

1 cup yogurt
1 clove garlic, crushed
1/2 tsp. ground ginger
salt and pepper to taste
1 frying chicken, cut up

Combine the first 4 ingredients in a bowl and marinate the chicken for at least 2 hours, turning at least once. Coat the chicken in flour, cornmeal or crushed corn flakes, and arrange in a lightly oiled baking pan. Bake at 350° for about an hour or until chicken is done and crisp on the outside.

CHICKEN IN CAPER SAUCE

3 tbsp. butter
1 broiling chicken, cut in quarters
1 tsp. salt
1 tbsp. flour
3/4 cup dry white wine
4 anchovy fillets, diced fine
2 tbsp. capers, drained
2 tbsp. lemon juice

Melt half the butter in a large skillet and brown the chicken well. Salt the chicken and remove it to a platter. Reduce heat and add flour, stirring until smooth and brown. Add wine, anchovies, capers and lemon juice. Stir in remaining butter. Return chicken to the skillet, cover, and cook over low heat half an hour or until tender. Turn the chicken once or twice while cooking.

By and large I don't like chicken dishes in which pieces of chicken with bone and skin still attached are dressed with a sauce. Too much sauce gets lost among the bones. You can make these next three dishes with chicken parts intact but they are nicer and easier to eat if the chicken parts are boned and skinned first.

PERSIAN CHICKEN

1/4 cup flour
1/2 tsp. salt
1/4 tsp. cumin powder
1/2 tsp. cracked black pepper
4 chicken breasts, skin and bones removed
3 tbsp. oil
3/4 cup dry white wine
1 cup rice or cracked wheat (bulgur)

2 *tbsp. onion, finely diced (tender green scallion tops are even better)*
2 *tbsp. butter*
1 *cup chicken broth*
1 *tsp. salt*
generous pinch oregano
1 *green pepper, seeded and cut into small strips*
1 *banana, cut into 1/4-in. slices*
1/2 *cup sour cream*

Combine flour, salt, cumin and pepper in a paper bag. Shake the chicken breasts in the bag until they are well coated. Heat a large skillet, put in the oil, and brown the chicken on both sides. Reduce the heat; add the wine, cover, and simmer until tender—about 20 minutes.

While the chicken is simmering, sauté the rice and onions in butter until rice begins to look transparent and onions are golden. Add chicken broth, salt and oregano. Bring this mixture to a boil, stirring well. Let boil one full minute, give a last stir and reduce heat to *very* low, and cover tightly. Do not disturb rice for 15 minutes. Then arrange the chicken on the rice and put in oven to stay warm (200°).

Cook the green pepper in the chicken drippings, adding a little water if the pan is too dry. Simmer the peppers until they are limp, and sprinkle them over the chicken. Sauté the banana slices in the skillet until they are heated through and arrange them among the chicken breasts. Stir the sour cream into the skillet and heat on a very low flame. When sour cream is hot, pour into a pitcher and serve with the chicken and rice.

CHICKEN CACCIATORE

1 frying chicken, cut up
3 tbsp. flour
1/2 tsp. salt
1/8 tsp. ground black pepper
salad oil as needed
2 garlic cloves, crushed
1/2 tsp. basil leaves, crumbled
1/2 tsp. oregano, crumbled
1 pt. tomatoes
1 green pepper, seeded and cut in chunks
5 or 6 mushrooms, sliced (optional)

Dredge the chicken in the flour, salt and pepper. Heat a large skillet and brown the chicken pieces in the oil, removing them as they are ready to a warm platter. Moisten the drippings in the pan with a little water; heat and stir until the drippings have dissolved. Add garlic, basil, oregano, tomatoes and pepper. Add the chicken; cover the skillet and let the chicken cook slowly for about half an hour. Five minutes before serving, sprinkle mushroom slices on top of the chicken and drizzle the dish lightly with sherry.

CHICKEN WITH OLIVE SAUCE

This is very good served with rice. This recipe will serve 6 nicely.

2 frying chickens, cut up
1 large onion, chopped
1 green pepper, seeded and chopped
15 stuffed green olives, chopped
2 tsp. salt
1/8 tsp. cinnamon, scant
1 tsp. cracked black peppercorns

1 tsp. coriander seeds, cracked in mortar
2 slices dry white bread, cut into small cubes
4 cups water, more if needed
1/2 pt. tomato purée
1/4 cup yellow raisins, plumped in warm water
10 slices stuffed olives, to garnish

Put the chicken, onion, green pepper, olives, spices and bread in a large saucepan or kettle. Add the water; cover and simmer until the chicken is tender—about 40 minutes. Add a little more water if there is danger of the mixture becoming too dry. Remove the chicken; add tomato purée and raisins, and heat the sauce. Remove skin and bones from the chicken and return meat to the kettle. Stir and heat. Pour chicken and sauce into a serving dish and garnish with sliced olives.

CHICKEN IN RED WINE

This is nice to have in early summer with little red potatoes boiled in their jackets and a green leafy salad.

1 plump frying chicken or 2 thin ones
salt and pepper
2 lemon wedges
4 tbsp. bacon fat
1-1/2 oz. cognac or brandy
1 bottle dry red wine
3 tbsp. grated carrot
pinch of garlic
pinch of thyme
15–20 small onions
1/2 cup sliced mushrooms
3 tbsp. butter

Cut the chicken into quarters and rub with salt, pepper and lemon. Heat a large, heavy skillet; melt bacon fat and brown the chicken well on both sides. Pour the cognac over the chicken and light it. Shake the pan gently until the flames go out. Pour in the red wine. Add the grated carrot, garlic and thyme. Cover and simmer about half an hour or until chicken is tender. The carrot will almost disappear, but will give the illusion of sweetness and body to the sauce.

Boil the onions until tender. Sauté mushrooms in butter. When chicken is tender, pour the wine sauce into a small saucepan and simmer onions and mushrooms in it a few minutes. Arrange the chicken on a heated platter and pour some of the sauce over the chicken; serve the rest in a gravy boat.

A plump stewing hen provides meat and stock for a variety of dishes. Cut the bird into quarters, and cook in water to cover in a covered kettle until the meat comes easily from the bones. Remove the chicken and set aside to cool. Skim the stock and refrigerate or freeze for use later in soups or sauces. Remove and discard the skin, bones and cartilage from the chicken and refrigerate the meat at once.

Use large pieces of white and dark meat that slice nicely in dishes where they show—hot and cold sandwiches, and chicken in sour cream. Use up leftovers and small pieces from the wings and neck in soups, mousses, creamed chicken and quickly prepared quasi-oriental concoctions.

CHICKEN IN SOUR CREAM

1 large breast of stewing chicken
leafy tops of 3 stalks of celery, chopped
1 large onion, chopped
5 peppercorns, coarsely cracked
1/2 tsp. salt
1-1/2 cups wide egg noodles
1 large onion, very thinly sliced

2 *tbsp. butter*
1 *cup sour cream*
1/2 *cup dry white wine*

Stew the chicken breasts with celery, chopped onion, pepper and salt until tender. Remove the chicken; strain the broth and boil the noodles in it until they are tender but not mushy—about 8 minutes. Drain the noodles and pour them into a shallow buttered baking dish. Skin and bone the chicken. Slice the meat and arrange it on the noodles. Sauté the sliced onion in the butter until soft; add the sour cream and wine. Simmer this sauce on a low heat about 10 minutes, stirring more frequently as it thickens. Salt to taste. Pour sauce over the chicken and noodles. Cover the casserole with lid or foil and heat in a 350° oven for 20 minutes, which is time enough to fix a salad and set the table.

CHICKEN SOUP

4 *cups chicken broth*
1 *bay leaf*
salad oil
2 *oz. (more or less) vermicelli or spaghettini (1/4 of 8-oz. package)*
meat from back, wings, neck and drumsticks of cooked stewing chicken
1 *tbsp. parsley, finely chopped*
1/2 *cup sliced raw mushrooms or 1/2 cup raw avocado chunks (optional)*
salt to taste

Heat broth with bay leaf in a large saucepan. Heat a skillet; pour in enough salad oil to coat the bottom, and add pasta, broken into short pieces. Cook and stir until noodles turn a golden color.

Bring the broth to a boil and add the fried pasta. Cook

about 5 minutes or until tender. Shred the chicken into the soup. Reduce heat and add the parsley, and mushrooms or avocado, if you have them. Let simmer 2 or 3 minutes—just long enough to let vegetables heat thoroughly but not cook. Fish out the bay leaf, salt to taste, and serve.

CHICKEN CORN SOUP I

This is a lightweight soup, comparatively speaking. It will serve 4 nicely and, with homemade biscuits or rolls and a salad, is a fine luncheon dish.

> 1 qt. chicken stock
> all the meat from stewing chicken except breast, thighs
>   and drumsticks
> 1 cup egg noodles (1/2 cup if homemade fresh noodles)
> 3 ears fresh corn or 1 cup canned cream-style corn
> 1 tsp. parsley, chopped fine
> 1 sprig marjoram
> salt and pepper to taste
> 2 hardboiled eggs, peeled and chopped

Heat the stock and meat in a kettle. If you use commercial egg noodles, boil them 5 minutes in salted water before adding to the broth; drop fresh homemade noodles directly into the boiling broth. Cut the corn from the cobs and let it boil in the soup 3 minutes. Remove the kettle from heat and add parsley, marjoram, salt and pepper. Pour soup into individual bowls; sprinkle grated egg on top and serve at once.

CHICKEN CORN SOUP II
(a main dish)

This is the most filling soup I know. If you sample the seven sweets and seven sours and have a cup of chicken corn soup at the beginning of a Pennsylvania Dutch dinner, it is doubtful you will be able to do justice to the main course. I

like to use this chicken corn soup as the main course—
especially in summer, when all the ingredients are fresh at
hand and it is so easy to fix side dishes of squash, cabbage
and fried peppers. This recipe serves 6.

> *1 stewing chicken (about 5 lbs.)*
> *1/2 cup celery, chopped*
> *1 medium onion, chopped*
> *1 tbsp. parsley, chopped*
> *pinch saffron*
> *pinch nutmeg*
> *9 or 10 ears corn, cut from the cob*
> *salt and pepper*
> *butter rivels (see below)*

Stew the chicken; strain the broth and remove bones, skin
and gristle from chicken. Cut the meat into small pieces and
return to the broth. Add celery, onion, parsley, saffron, nutmeg and corn. Let boil 3 minutes. Salt and pepper to taste.
Add the rivels; cover tightly and cook 8 minutes. Serve at
once.

BUTTER RIVELS

> *2 tbsp. soft butter*
> *3/4 cup flour*
> *1/2 tsp. salt*
> *milk*

Cut butter, flour and salt together with 2 knives or a pastry
blender. Add as little milk as possible, just enough to bind
the dough. Form into small balls the size of a hazel nut. Refrigerate until needed.

CHICKEN AMERISINO

This approximation of a Chinese chicken and vegetable
dish is fast and economical to prepare—especially in summer.

I put the rice on first and fix the chicken while the rice is cooking. I usually make this when there are guests in the house. Even non-cooking guests can slice onions, dice celery and pick snow peas, thus freeing me to prepare side dishes and dessert—salads, a vegetable, strawberries or peaches. You can fancy this dish up with bamboo shoots, water chestnuts and slivered almonds, but it is then no longer very economical.

Much experimenting has been done: carrots, cabbage and tomatoes do not go well with the other vegetables. The tomato adds a nice color but is too shapeless when cooked compared to the peppers, chard and snow peas that retain their form. A red pepper instead of green goes nicely, or a few strips of pimiento if you have some on hand. Pineapple chunks are too harsh a flavor but pineapple juice substituted for half the water in the sauce is subtle and very good.

Serve the chicken with rice and accompany it with a fresh cucumber salad, cherry tomatoes, carrot sticks, pickled eggs, steamed cabbage with vinegar, etc.

> oil
> 1 *green pepper, seeded and chopped coarsely*
> 1 *stalk celery, sliced on a slant*
> 2 *stalks Swiss chard, cut like the celery or 1/2 cup snow peas or 1 can bean sprouts, well drained*
> 1 *medium onion, coarsely chopped*
> 1 *clove garlic, cut in half*
> 2 *thin slices of fresh ginger root*
> 1 *tbsp. cornstarch*
> 1 *cup water*
> salt *and* pepper *to taste*
> 1 *tbsp. soy sauce*
> 1 *cup cooked chicken, cut in bite-size pieces*
> 1/2 *lb. (1 cup) sliced mushrooms (optional)*

Heat a large skillet and put in enough oil to cover bottom. Stir-fry quickly the pepper and celery. When they begin to soften, add the chard or snow peas, onion, garlic and ginger. Stir-fry 1 minute longer. Combine cornstarch and water; add this to the vegetables and stir until liquid clears. Reduce heat to very low and add salt, pepper and soy sauce. Taste and add more of these seasonings if needed. At this point you can cover the dish, remove it from the heat and let it sit awhile if you have other things to do. When you are ready, return the skillet to the heat and stir in the chicken, bean sprouts (if you are using them) and mushrooms, which should merely be heated, rather than thoroughly cooked.

HOT CHICKEN LOAF

> 3 cups chicken meat, very finely diced or put through blender
> 1 medium onion, very finely chopped
> 2 eggs
> 3/4 cup cream or whole milk
> 1-1/2 cups breadcrumbs or leftover cooked rice
> 1 tsp. lemon juice
> pinch nutmeg
> salt and pepper to taste

Combine all ingredients in a bowl and mix very thoroughly. Pack in a 1-1/2-quart pan and cover securely with lid or foil. Place in a larger pan and pour 1 inch hot water around it. Bake at 350° for 1 hour, when the loaf should be set and firm. Slice and serve with a sauce.

MUSTARD SAUCE

> 1/2 cup mayonnaise
> 1/2 cup sour cream
> 2 tbsp. prepared mustard

Combine the 3 ingredients in a small bowl; mix well and salt to taste.

WATERCRESS AND PARSLEY SAUCE

2 *tbsp. butter*
2 *tbsp. flour*
1 *cup chicken stock*
10–12 *sprigs watercress*
3 *sprigs parsley*
1/2 *cup cream*
salt

Combine butter and flour in a small saucepan, and heat and mix until they are completely blended. Add the chicken stock slowly, blending as you pour. Let this base simmer, stirring occasionally, about 15 minutes, by which time it will be somewhat reduced. Meanwhile, immerse the cress and parsley briefly (less than 1 minute) in boiling water. Shake dry in a basket or muslin bag, and chop as finely as possible. Add the cress and parsley and cream to the stock. Simmer very gently about 10 minutes longer; salt to taste and serve in a gravy boat.

CHICKEN CROQUETTES

I love croquettes but after working in a number of restaurants, I'm afraid to eat them anywhere but home.

7 *slices white bread*
3 *tbsp. milk*
1 *medium onion, finely minced*
2 *tbsp. butter*
2 *cups cooked chicken, chopped*
1 *egg*
salt and pepper
1 *egg beaten with 2 tbsp. water*
1 *cup breadcrumbs*
4 *tbsp. butter*

Remove the crusts from the bread and soak bread in milk. Sauté onion in butter until soft but do not let it brown. Squeeze the bread dry and mix with chicken, egg, onion, salt and pepper. Shape mixture into croquettes and let dry 10 minutes. Dip croquettes in the egg mixture and roll them in crumbs. Melt the 4 tbsp. butter and fry the croquettes until they form crusts, then reduce heat and cook the croquettes until they are done. This is most easily done by putting them in a shallow baking dish and baking them in a 300° oven for 20 to 30 minutes. Meanwhile, make a sauce by pouring 1 cup chicken stock or beef stock and 1 tbsp. butter into the pan in which the croquettes were fried; cook and stir until scrapings are incorporated into the sauce.

CREAMED CHICKEN TART

Leftover chicken is easily made into creamed chicken, which can be served over rice, toast, kasha or bulgur. For something a little special, serve creamed chicken in this rich tart shell.

Dough

1/2 cup cream cheese (8-oz. package)
1/2 cup butter
1 cup flour (a little more if needed)
1/2 tsp. sugar

Blend cheese and butter; add flour and sugar. Knead until smooth. Wrap dough in wax paper and chill 12 hours. Roll dough out on a floured board, and make a pie shell and a lid. Bake at 400° until brown (about 15 minutes).

CREAMED CHICKEN

2 *tbsp. flour*
2 *tbsp. butter*
1 *cup cream*
1/2 *tsp. salt*
1-1/2 *cups cooked chicken, diced*
2 *tbsp. cooked carrot, finely diced*
1/4 *cup peas, blanched, or leftover cooked peas*
4 *strips pimiento, diced*
1 *egg yolk*

In the top part of a double boiler, combine the flour and butter; cook and stir until blended. Add cream gradually, stirring constantly. Add salt, chicken, carrot, peas and pimiento. Put pan over simmering water and stir in egg yolk to thicken. Pour creamed chicken into the tart shell when it comes out of the oven. Put the lid on and serve.

SHERRIED CREAM CHICKEN

This approximation of Lobster Newburg is easy to fix and rich. Crabmeat is good instead of or in combination with the chicken. Tuna fish is not good. Serve over buttered toast cut in squares. This recipe serves 2 generously.

1 *tbsp. flour*
1 *tbsp. butter*
1 *cup cream or whole milk*
salt and pepper
dash cayenne powder or tabasco sauce
1/2 *tsp. paprika*
1 *tbsp. sherry*
3/4 *cup chicken or crabmeat or a combination of the two*
2 *egg yolks*

Combine the flour and butter; blend and cook. Gradually stir in the milk. Salt and pepper to taste; add cayenne or tabasco, paprika and sherry. Put the pan over simmering water and stir in the meat and egg yolks.

MEAT FOR BREAKFAST

Bacon, ham, sausage and scrapple are standard breakfast fare. We all know how to deal with bacon and ham. Sausage is best done under the broiler. Horseradish is a good traditional sauce for sausage. Equally good is "cocktail sauce"— a combination of ketchup and horseradish. A good and slightly different sauce consists of 1 egg yolk beaten lightly, to which is added 1 tsp. soy sauce, 2 tbsp. ketchup and 3 tbsp. horseradish. Mix well and serve. It is best to prepare this quietly in the kitchen with no onlookers, since some people are squeamish about raw egg early in the day.

SCRAPPLE (PANNHAAS)

Scrapple should be fried on a grill or in a pan that is lightly greased. Do not cover scrapple or it will steam and fall apart. Turn scrapple when you can see a brown crust along the bottom of each slice. Turned too soon, it falls apart and presents an unappetizing appearance. Fresh bread and butter with marmalade or jam go well with scrapple. In the Philadelphia area at least it is not unusual to see people pouring maple syrup over it.

Good scrapple is scarce even in the Philadelphia-to-Harrisburg area. It is economical and easy to make, and takes little extra time on a soup-making and baking day. The next recipe is for those close enough to the country or a real butcher shop to obtain the pig parts needed. The other two scrapples can be prepared by anyone.

SCRAPPLE No. 1

1 hog's head, eyes and brain removed
1 pork liver
1 pork heart
4 pig's feet, scraped
water
sage
salt
ground black pepper to taste
cornmeal as needed
buckwheat flour as needed

Cut the hog's head in half; wash it well in cold water and put it in a large kettle. Add the liver, heart and pig's feet. Add water to cover and bring to a boil. Skim off the scum, cover the kettle and simmer for about 3 hours, when the meat will be falling from the bones. Discard the bones and gristle. Chop the meat finely and strain the broth. Add 1/2 tsp. sage, 1 tbsp. salt and 1 tsp. pepper. Simmer the broth while you prepare the meat and meal.

Weigh the meat and for every 3 lbs. of meat, measure 2 lbs. of either cornmeal or buckwheat flour, or a combination of the two. Return the meat to the broth; bring to a boil and sift in the meal gradually, stirring constantly so that the mixture is smooth. Taste and adjust seasonings. Reduce the heat and cook over a low heat, stirring frequently. The mixture will now be the consistency of a soft mush. Rinse loaf pans in cold water. Pour in the scrapple and let set. Refrigerate as soon as scrapple is lukewarm.

SCRAPPLE No. 2

This recipe is very easy and can be made by anyone. It yields about 2 bread-loaf pans of scrapple.

2 lbs. lean pork scraps and meaty bones
water
salt and pepper to taste
1/2 tsp. ground sage
1/8 tsp. mace
3/4 cup buckwheat flour
3/4 cup cornmeal

Put the pork in a kettle with water to cover; salt and pepper lightly, and simmer until the meat falls from the bones. Skim the fat from the broth; strain the broth and add the sage and mace. Discard the bones. Chop the meat finely and add it to the broth. Bring to a boil and sift in the cornmeal and buckwheat flour. If the mixture is less than liquid at this point, add 1 cup water. Simmer and stir to thicken for 1 hour. Adjust seasonings. Rinse loaf pans in cold water and pour scrapple into them. Let set. Slice and fry, or refrigerate for later use.

OATMEAL SCRAPPLE

This spicy scrapple is as suitable to the dinner table as to brunch or breakfast.

1 medium onion coarsely chopped
1 bay leaf
1 tbsp. coarsely cracked black pepper
2 lbs. lean pork trimmings and meaty bones
water
1 cup oatmeal
1 tsp. salt
1/8 tsp. nutmeg
1/8 tsp. cayenne powder
1 tbsp. grated onion
1/4 tsp. dried thyme

Put onion, bay leaf and black pepper in kettle with pork and water to cover. Simmer the pork for two hours or until meat falls from bones. Strain the broth into a heavy saucepan and cook to reduce to 2-1/2 cups. Add the oatmeal and salt and let boil for 3 minutes, stirring constantly. Reduce heat and let the mixture simmer for 15 minutes.

Remove the meat from the bones and chop finely. Combine the oatmeal mixture, the meat, nutmeg, cayenne, grated onion and thyme in a bowl, and mix well. Adjust salt to taste. Pack in 2 bread-loaf pans and chill at least 6 hours before slicing and frying.

GROUND BEEF

As the finer cuts of meat move rapidly into the luxury category, more and more space in print is being devoted to ground beef dishes. I confine my remarks mainly to meatballs and pirogis.

Meatballs in tomato gravy make spaghetti a main dish. Ladled into a fresh roll, they make a hearty sandwich filling. It is essential to use fresh ingredients. Onion flakes, dried parsley, garlic powder and breadcrumbs will result in hard, dry meatballs. This recipe makes about 30 walnut-sized meatballs and a small meatloaf that will serve two generously.

> 3 *lbs. ground meat (equal parts of veal, pork and beef is ideal but expensive; ground chuck alone often has to do)*
> 3 *cloves garlic, very finely chopped*
> 2 *medium onions, very finely chopped*
> 1/2 *cup (loosely packed) fresh parsley leaves, finely chopped*
> 4 *slices Italian or French bread, soaked in water and squeezed dry*
> 2 *eggs, lightly beaten*
> 1 *tbsp. oregano*

1-1/2 tsp. salt
generous pinch ground black pepper

Combine all ingredients in a large bowl and mix thoroughly, but as lightly as possible, with a fork. Heat a large skillet and pour in vegetable oil to coat the bottom generously. Fry one small meatball and taste. Add salt to the meat mixture if necessary. Fry the meatballs over a moderate flame until they are nicely browned on all sides. With a slotted spoon, remove the meatballs from the skillet and put them into the kettle of simmering tomato gravy (p. 31), where they will continue cooking.

Pack a small loaf pan with the meat mixture and wrap in freezer paper; seal, date and freeze for future use.

SPICY MEATBALLS IN CREAM

Serve with steamed brown rice (p. 65) and a green salad to feed 5 nicely for lunch or dinner.

1 lb. ground round steak or chuck
1/2 lb. ground lean pork
1 egg, slightly beaten
1/2 cup mashed potatoes
1/2 cup breadcrumbs
1/2 cup milk
1-1/2 tsp. salt
1/2 tsp. ginger
generous pinch nutmeg
1/4 tsp. ground black pepper
flour as needed (1/4 cup should be enough)
vegetable oil
1 cup cream

Combine the meats, egg, potatoes, breadcrumbs, milk and spices in a large bowl and mix thoroughly. Shape into walnut-

sized meatballs. Dredge lightly in the flour. Heat enough
vegetable oil to cover the skillet bottom and brown the meatballs quickly on all sides. Do not turn your back on them
because if they scorch, the flavor of the entire dish will be
tainted. As soon as they have browned, spoon them into a
casserole. Set the casserole in a shallow pan of water, pour
the cream over the meatballs, and cover the casserole. Bake
about 40 minutes.

SWEET AND SOUR MEATBALLS

Very good with pilau. Serves 5.

> *1/2 cup dry breadcrumbs*
> *1/2 cup milk*
> *1 medium onion, very finely chopped*
> *1-1/2 lbs. ground chuck*
> *1/2 cup parsley, finely minced (loosely packed)*
> *1 scant tsp. dried mint flakes or 1 tbsp. fresh mint, very*
> *finely chopped*
> *1 egg*
> *1 clove garlic, very finely chopped*
> *1-1/2 tsp. salt*
> *generous pinch ground black pepper*
> *vegetable oil*
> *3 tbsp. vinegar*
> *1 tbsp. brown sugar*
> *oregano or finely minced parsley to garnish*

In a large bowl, soak the breadcrumbs in the milk. Mix well
and add onion, meat, parsley, mint, egg, garlic, salt and
pepper. Mix thoroughly and form into small meatballs. Heat
enough oil to cover the bottom of the skillet and brown the
meatballs on all sides, cooking them thoroughly. Spoon the
meatballs onto a heated serving dish. Combine the vinegar
and sugar in the skillet and stir over a low heat to incorporate
the drippings into the sauce and completely dissolve the

sugar. Pour this sauce over the meatballs, garnish with oregano or parsley, and serve.

PIROGI

Serve pirogi as a main dish for dinner or lunch. Bite-size pirogi are ideal for brunches, teas or parties. You can use a standard bread dough, the richer cottage cheese-and-butter dough, or a container of prepared roll mix from the supermarket.

DOUGH

> 1 *cake yeast* or *1 envelope dried yeast*
> 1 *cup lukewarm milk*
> 5 *cups flour*
> 3 *eggs*
> 1 *tsp. sugar*
> 1 *tsp. salt*
> 1/4 *lb. butter, melted*

Dissolve the yeast in the milk. Stir in 1 cup flour and let the mixture stand in a warm place for 1 hour. Beat eggs, sugar, salt and butter together and stir into the yeast mixture. Sift in the remaining 4 cups flour, stirring at first, then kneading when the dough becomes stiff. Form the dough into a ball and put into a greased bowl to rise. When double in size, the dough is ready to use.

COTTAGE CHEESE DOUGH

> 8 *oz. cottage cheese*
> 1/4 *lb. butter*
> 1 *cup flour, approximately (if cottage cheese is very liquid, more flour may be needed)*
> 1/2 *tsp. sugar*
> 1/4 *tsp. salt*

Combine the cheese and butter with 2 knives or a pastry blender. When a smooth paste is achieved, add the flour, sugar and salt. Knead until smooth. Wrap the dough in waxed paper and chill overnight.

PIROGI FILLING

1 *medium head cabbage, preferably white and tender*
3 *large onions*
2 *tbsp. oil*
1 *lb. ground chuck*
salt and pepper
dough
egg white

Slice the cabbage and onions thinly. Sauté them gently in the oil until tender. Push the vegetables to one side and brown the chuck in the center of the skillet. Mix the meat and vegetables together, salt and pepper to taste, and let cool.

Pinch off small piece of dough and roll out on a floured board to make sheets about 5 inches square. Put a generous tbsp. of filling in the center of each, and fold over the corners of the dough so that when the pirogi is turned over it looks like a tiny, smooth loaf of bread. Pinch the dough edges together. Place the pirogi on a greased baking sheet, brush the tops with beaten white of egg, and bake at 400° for 20 minutes or until nicely browned on top. This recipe yields about 25 small pirogi.

STOVE-TOP STEW

When you are pressed to provide an instant meal on short notice with very little meat, a pound of chuck can go a very long way. This concoction, lacking in subtlety though it may be, is popular in my house. The seasonings, the colorfulness of the vegetables, and the carrot-enriched broth help to obscure the fact that meat is in short supply. A little red wine added to the sauce in the last few minutes is very good. I serve this in soup bowls over freshly steamed or leftover rice or over egg noodles.

> 1 lb. ground chuck
> 2 medium onions, coarsely chopped
> vegetable oil
> 2 medium tomatoes, coarsely chopped
> 2 green peppers, finely chopped
> 1 tbsp. soy sauce
> 2 tbsp. grated carrot
> salt to taste
> 1 tsp. oregano
> 1 tsp. cornstarch
> 1/2 cup water or tomato juice

Brown the chuck and onions, in enough oil to cover the bottom of the skillet, over a moderate flame. Stir frequently to prevent sticking. Add the tomatoes and peppers and let cook 2 minutes. Add soy sauce, grated carrot, salt and oregano. Combine the cornstarch and water and add gradually to the mixture, stirring and cooking until a medium-thick gravy results. Add an ounce of dry red wine if you like. Stir once or twice and serve.

ODDS AND ENDS

Flavor for meat and gravy. I keep a jar of this preparation on the stove shelf all winter long. A sprinkle or two flavors roasts nicely and it serves as an ever-ready marinade.

1 large onion, diced
1 tbsp. red pepper flakes or 1 fresh hot pepper, chopped
2 tbsp. brown sugar
1 tsp. celery seed
1 tsp. cracked mustard seed
1 tbsp. cracked peppercorns

Put all ingredients into a quart bottle and fill with vinegar. Keep corked and use as needed.

Clarifying lard to use either in cooking or to seal crocks. Heat lard to 180° and allow it to cool slowly. When the lard is lukewarm, strain it through 2 or 3 layers of cheesecloth. The cheesecloth will strain out foreign matter and, as the lard cools, any water will precipitate beneath it. When lard is completely cool, remove it and store in airtight containers in a cool place until needed.

CHAPTER 5

Pickles and Preserves

*P*ICKLES, relishes, chutnies, jams and jellies are luxuries at today's prices. Made at home, they become economical, using to good advantage the surplus of the garden to enliven budget-conscious winter meals. Unusual preserves like quince honey, dill cherry tomatoes and red pepper jam are often not available commercially and make distinctive hostess and housewarming gifts, as well as prized contributions to P.T.A. bake sales and church bazaars.

August and the first half of September are the busiest season for the home pickler and preserver. Time is in short supply at this time of year: the garden needs tending, meals and routine household tasks require attention, the kitchen is in chaos, and it is hot. Organization is the key to successful and enjoyable preserving. Pick or buy the fruits and vegetables the evening before a day of canning. To do this on the morning of a canning day means that it will be at least 10 A.M. before you are ready to begin and guarantees that you will be in the kitchen through the hottest part of the day.

Get up early enough that breakfast is over and the kitchen cleaned up by no later than 5 A.M. Between 5 and 10 A.M. you can make three or four batches of pickles and preserves. With a good job well done, you will still have time to take a shower and prepare lunch by noon. Clean up as you work. Colanders, food mills, strainers and funnels should go into a large pan of soapy water the minute you have finished with them. Wash them while the preserves are cooking. If food particles are permitted to dry on these utensils, cleaning becomes tedious and time consuming.

The following are my favorite pickle and preserve recipes. Most of them are quite simply and easily made. Quite a few require no water for the cooking of the ingredients. In many areas homemade pickles and preserves may turn a disappointing dark, drab color. Often the fault lies in the water. Fluoride, chlorine and other minerals can greatly affect the color and clarity of pickles and their brine.

In using these or other pickling recipes you will obtain the best results by using distilled white vinegar and pure granulated salt, both of which are often available in supermarkets and "health food" stores. Pickling salt, prepared brines and spices are often sold, by the gallons and pounds, by pickling companies at prices considerably lower than in the supermarket. Dark vinegars may produce dark pickles and relishes. Ordinary table salt sometimes contains lump-preventing additives that can affect color and texture. Use whole spices rather than powders for clearer brines and brighter colors.

After you have packed the pickles in the jars and covered them with brine, you will often notice air bubbles in the jars. Before putting on the sealer lid and ring, run the sterilized blade of a table knife around the inside of the jar until all the air bubbles have escaped.

Be sure to label all your pickles and preserves. If you have made a new recipe or tried a variation of an old favorite, mark at least one jar with the source of the recipe or a note of the change you made in ingredients or proportions. Otherwise you may not be able to duplicate the recipe in future. You will save time and annoyance if you put the labels on the sealer lids of the jars intended for home use instead of on the jars themselves. I find that, although the labels I put on jars for sale or for gifts often partially or wholly refuse to stick, the ones for home use usually stick so well that they defy soap and water, soaking and the brush, and often have to be removed with a razor blade. Since the sealer lid is only used once, the label is discarded each year and cleaning the jars presents no problem.

CUCUMBER PICKLES

BREAD AND BUTTER PICKLES—PAT'S FAVORITE

8 *cups cucumbers, sliced thin*
5 *tbsp (approx.) salt*
2 *cups onions, sliced thin*
4 *green peppers, chopped fine*
2 *cups vinegar*
3 *cups sugar*
2 *tsp. celery seed*
3 *tsp. turmeric*
3-inch cinnamon stick

Sprinkle the cucumbers with salt and let stand 1 hour. Drain the cucumbers and combine with the rest of the ingredients in a large, heavy-bottomed pot. Boil gently for 20 minutes, stirring frequently. Ladle into hot jars and seal.

Yield: 3–4 pints.

QUICK CUCUMBER PICKLES

6 qts. sliced cucumbers (to 1/4 inch thick)
6 medium onions, sliced
1/2 cup salt
1 qt. vinegar
6 cups sugar
1/2 tsp. cayenne pepper
2 oz. mustard seed (1 small package)
1 tbsp. celery seed

Sprinkle the cucumbers and onions with salt; let stand 3 hours. Drain well. Boil the vinegar, sugar, pepper, mustard and celery seed for 5 minutes. Put the cucumber and onion slices into this syrup and heat until the mixture is just about to boil. Ladle into hot, sterilized jars and seal.

Yield: 8 pints.

SWEET CUCUMBER PICKLE CHIPS

4 lbs. cucumbers
4 cups vinegar
3 tbsp. salt
1 tbsp. mustard seed
2-1/2 cups vinegar
6 cups sugar
2 tsp. celery seed
1 tbsp. allspice

Cut cucumbers into chips (about 1/4-inch-thick slices). In a good-size pot, combine them with the 4 cups vinegar, salt and mustard seed. Cook gently for 10 minutes. Drain the cucumbers and discard the liquid. Pack the cucumbers in hot jars. Combine the 2-1/2 cups vinegar with the sugar, celery seed and allspice, and heat to boiling, making sure that the sugar is thoroughly dissolved. Fill the jars with the hot syrup to 1/4 inch from the top. Seal each jar the minute it is filled.

Yield: 4 pints.

SWEET GHERKINS

4 qts. gherkins
1 gal. water
1 cup salt
11 cups sugar
2 qts. vinegar
2 tbsp. whole allspice
2 tbsp. whole cloves
2 tbsp. mustard seed
1 tbsp. celery seed
1 stick cinnamon (about 4 inches long)
4 bay leaves

Soak the gherkins overnight or for 12 hours in a brine made of the water and salt. Drain the gherkins and rinse them in fresh water. Combine the sugar and vinegar in a large pot, and bring to a boil. Add the gherkins and spices. Let it all simmer 5 minutes, then remove the pot from the heat and let cool. Pack the pickles in jars. Reheat the syrup to the boiling point. Fill the jars and seal.

Yield: 7 pints.

ANNA'S AMISH PICKLES (7-DAY PICKLES)

7 lbs. cucumbers
1 qt. cider vinegar
8 cups sugar
2 tbsp. salt
2 tbsp. pickling spices or 1 tbsp. each mustard **and** allspice

Scrub the cucumbers and put them in a crock. Cover them with boiling water. Repeat the scrubbing and the hot water treatment once a day for 4 days, keeping the cucumbers in the crock covered with a clean cloth between treatments. On the 5th day, cut the cucumbers into slices, chunks or spears. Boil the rest of the ingredients together and pour the syrup over the pickles. On the 6th day, pour off the syrup, bring it to a boil and pour again over the pickles. On the 7th day, pour off the syrup, bring it to a boil, add the pickles, bring to a boil, and pack them into hot jars and seal.

CUMBERLAND COUNTY DILL PICKLES

This is a real country recipe designed to put up whatever number of cucumbers you may have.

> *cucumbers*
> *vinegar*
> *salt*
> *dill*
> *bay leaves*
> *peppercorns*
> *garlic cloves (if you like)*

Wash the cucumbers well, cut them into spears and pack them in jars. Fill the jars 3/4 full of cold water, and fill the rest of the way with vinegar. Pour all the liquid from all the jars into a pot, add 2 tbsp. salt for each quart of pickles, and bring this brine to a boil. Pour over the pickles and let cool until the next day. Pour off liquid again; bring it to a boil, adding a good pinch of each of the spices. Pour the liquid over the pickles and seal the jars.

RIPE CUCUMBER PICKLES

If you have your own garden, you are almost certain to have cucumbers that turn yellow before they can be used—

especially at the end of the season. This recipe is a good way to prevent their going to waste.

>6 *large ripe cucumbers*
>1/4 *cup salt*
>1 *cup sugar*
>2 *cups vinegar*
>1/2 *cup water*
>1 *tbsp. whole allspice*
>1 *tbsp. mustard seed*
>1 *bay leaf*

Slice the cucumbers into a bowl; sprinkle them with salt and let them stand overnight or 12 hours. Drain well. Rinse under cold running water and drain again in a colander. Combine the rest of the ingredients in a good-sized pan and bring to a boil. Simmer the cucumbers in this syrup for 15 minutes. Pack into hot jars and seal.

Yield: 3–4 pints.

OTHER PICKLES

WATERMELON RIND PICKLE

>3 *lbs. watermelon rind*
>1 *gal. water*
>2 *tbsp. salt*
>5 *cups sugar*
>2 *cups vinegar*
>1 *cup water*
>1 *tbsp. allspice*
>1 *tbsp. whole cloves*
>1 *stick cinnamon*
>1 *lemon, sliced*

Remove any pink meat from the rind and cut rind into bite-size squares. Soak them overnight in the gallon of water with the salt. Drain. Cover with fresh water and boil until just tender. Drain. Mix the sugar, vinegar, 1 cup water; add the spices, in a cheesecloth bag, and the lemon slices. Boil this mixture 5 minutes. Add the rind and cook until the rind becomes transparent. Remove the spice bag and lemon slices. Ladle pickles into jars and fill with the syrup. A slightly fancier pickle can be made by putting one whole clove in each square of rind. If you do this, omit the cloves from the spice bag.

Yield: 6–8 pints.

MOCK WATERMELON PRESERVES

> 1 *pumpkin, 4–5 lbs.*
> *sugar–equal weight to prepared pumpkin*
> 2 *large lemons*

Peel the pumpkin and remove seeds and fibre from the center. Cut the pumpkin into small squares. Sprinkle the squares with their weight of sugar and let stand overnight. Drain off the syrup that forms and bring it to a boil in an agate or stainless steel pan. Add the lemon slices and the pumpkin and cook until the syrup thickens and the pumpkin is tender (usually about half an hour). Ladle into hot jars and seal.

Yield: About 8 pints.

PICKLED CRABAPPLES

These are a good garnish for pork dishes and make a good base for a sweet-and-sour barbecue sauce.

> 4 *qts. crabapples*
> 2 *cups vinegar*
> 5 *cups sugar*

1 tbsp. whole cloves
1 stick cinnamon (about 4 inches)
1 small piece of ginger root, washed and scraped

Wash the crabapples, remove the blossom end, and prick each apple with the tines of a fork. Do not peel. Combine the remaining ingredients in a saucepan and simmer 20 minutes. Add the crabapples a few at a time and simmer all until tender. Pack the apples in hot sterilized jars and add syrup to fill the jar. Seal.

Yield: About 6 pints.

PEPPER RINGS

A colorful, unusual gift and a good seller at bazaars. Excellent on steak sandwiches.

6 sweet green peppers
6 sweet red peppers
1-1/2 cups sugar
3 cups vinegar

Remove the tops, seeds and white membrane from the peppers and slice into 1/4-inch-wide rings. Cover the peppers with boiling water and let stand 2 minutes. Drain and pack in hot, sterile jars, preferably straight-sided. Have ready and hot a syrup made by boiling together the sugar and vinegar for 5 minutes. Pour syrup over the peppers to within 1/4 inch of the top of the jar. Seal.

Yield: 7–8 pints.

DILL CARROTS

2 qts. finger-length carrots
1 tbsp. mustard seed
2 tbsp. dill seed
2 cloves garlic
2-1/2 cups vinegar
2-1/2 cups water
3 tbsp. salt

Simmer the carrots in water until the skins slip off easily. Drain, remove skins, and pack into hot jars. Put a pinch of mustard seed and dill seed in each jar. Combine garlic, vinegar, water and salt in a separate pan, and heat to boiling. Remove garlic cloves and pour the hot liquid over the carrots, filling the jars to within 1/2 inch from the top. Seal and process in a boiling water bath for 5 minutes.

Yield: 4 pints.

SOUR DILL TOMATOES

3 qts. small green tomatoes
dill
garlic cloves
2 qts. water
1 cup vinegar
1/2 cup salt

Pack the clean tomatoes in jars, putting a few sprigs of dill and 1 garlic clove in each jar. Combine the water, vinegar and salt, and fill the jars with this brine. Seal and let stand for at least 3 months before using.

Yield: 6 pints.

RELISHES

Onions and hot peppers contain juices that sting and burn. Handle them as little as necessary. Be especially careful if you have any scratches on your hands. Use a wooden spoon to push onions and hot peppers into the food mill, or the tips of your fingers are certain to be scraped. A good dose of hot pepper juice can make your hands burn for as long as twelve hours. Do not touch your eyes or any tender skin area while working with onions and hot peppers. If possible, keep small children away from raw onions and hot peppers. Wash your hands carefully when you have finished. Put any cloths that may have raw juice, especially of hot peppers, in the laundry at once.

INDIA RELISH

8 or 10 green tomatoes
4 large onions
6 large green peppers
1/4 cup salt
3 tbsp. dry mustard
2 tbsp. ground ginger
3/4 cup sugar
1/2 tsp. ground cloves
1/2 tsp. ground allspice
2 tbsp. celery seed
1 qt. vinegar

Put the vegetables through the fine blade of the food mill. Combine the remaining ingredients in a large saucepan and simmer and stir until sugar and salt are dissolved. Add the chopped vegetables to the syrup and bring to a boil. Boil slowly for 30 minutes, stirring frequently. Ladle into hot, sterilized jars and seal.

Yield: About 6 pints.

COPLEY PLAZA RELISH

2 *lbs. green tomatoes (7 medium-size tomatoes)*
2 *lbs. ripe tomatoes (7 medium-size tomatoes)*
3 *red peppers*
2 *green peppers*
5 *medium onions*
1/4 *cup salt*
2 *cups sugar*
1-1/2 *cups vinegar*

Put the vegetables through the medium blade of the food mill. Make a syrup of the salt, sugar and vinegar. Add the chopped vegetables and cook 30 minutes. Pour into hot, sterilized jars and seal.

Yield: About 4 pints.

HAMBURG RELISH

36 *tomatoes*
12 *peppers*
15 *onions*
1 *qt. vinegar*
2 *cups sugar*
3 *tbsp. salt*
3 *tbsp. cinnamon*

Put the vegetables through the coarse blade of the food mill. Put the vegetables along with all the other ingredients into a large, heavy saucepan and boil slowly until the relish thickens, about 1-1/2 hours. Ladle into hot, sterilized jars and seal.

Yield: About 10 pints.

BALTIMORE RELISH

1 large head of cabbage, cored
12 large onions
4 green peppers
2 qts. chopped ripe tomatoes
2 qts. chopped green tomatoes
1/2 cup salt
2 qts. white vinegar
2 cloves garlic, pressed
1-1/2 lbs. sugar
1/2 cup white mustard seed
1/2 cup grated horseradish
1 tbsp. celery seed

Put the cabbage, onions and peppers through the coarse blade of the food mill and add to the chopped tomatoes. Mix the vegetables with the salt and let stand overnight. Drain. Add remaining ingredients and boil until relish thickens. Ladle into hot, sterilized jars and seal.

Yield: About 12 pints.

AUNT TILL'S CHILI SAUCE

12 large ripe tomatoes
2 large onions
4 green peppers
2 tbsp. salt
1/2 cup sugar
1 tsp. cinnamon
1 tsp. ground cloves
2-1/2 cups vinegar

Put tomatoes, onions and peppers through the coarse blade of the food mill. Cook slowly with the spices and vinegar until thick (usually 45 to 60 minutes). Stir occasionally.

Yield: About 4 pints.

SOUTH JERSEY CHOW CHOW

1 qt. shelled lima beans
2 qts. small onions
2 small heads cauliflower, broken into florets
12 green peppers
1 qt. green tomatoes
1 pt. sweet pickles
6 ears corn
2 lbs. sugar
2 tbsp. mustard seed
2 tbsp. celery seed
12 oz. prepared salad mustard (2 6-oz. jars)
1 pt. vinegar

Cook the limas, onions and cauliflower in salted water until almost tender. Drain. Chop the peppers, tomatoes and pickles coarsely. Cut the corn from the cob. Combine the raw vegetables in a large kettle. Add all the spices and cook, stirring frequently until the relish thickens slightly. Add the cooked, drained vegetables and cook until slightly thick. Ladle into hot, sterilized jars and seal.

Yield: 10–12 pints.

ONION RELISH

This is not available commercially, so far as I know. It is a little hot. If you are going to make gifts of onion relish or donate some to a church sale, be sure to note on the label that it is hot.

14 medium onions
6 green peppers
6 hot red peppers
3 cups sugar
4 cups white vinegar
2 tbsp. salt

Put the onions and peppers through the medium blade of the food mill. Turn them into a large bowl and cover with boiling water. Let stand 4 minutes. Drain well. In a saucepan, combine the sugar, vinegar and salt. Cook over a low flame until salt and sugar are dissolved. Add onions and peppers and boil gently for 15 minutes. Ladle into hot, sterilized jars and seal.

Yield: About 3 pints.

PEPPER RELISH

12 *red sweet peppers*
12 *green peppers*
12 *medium onions*
2 *cups vinegar*
1-1/2 *cups sugar*
2 *tbsp. salt*
1 *tbsp. celery seed*

Put the peppers and onions through the medium blade of the food mill. Put the chopped vegetables in a large bowl and cover with boiling water. Let stand 5 minutes. Drain. Combine the vinegar, sugar and spices in a saucepan and boil for 5 minutes. Add the vegetables and boil for 10 minutes. Pack in hot, sterilized jars and seal.

Yield: About 4-1/2 pints.

PEPPER HASH

Small dishes of this can serve as a substitute for salad in winter.

12 *green peppers*
12 *red sweet peppers*
8 *onions*
3 *cups hot cider vinegar*
1-1/2 *cups sugar*
1/2 *tsp. salt*

Put the peppers and onions through the fine blade of the food mill and then into a saucepan. Cover with the hot vinegar. Add the sugar and salt and stir well. Taste and add more salt if necessary. Bring the hash to a boil; reduce heat and simmer for 20 minutes. Pour into hot, sterilized jars and seal.

Yield: About 2 pints.

SWEET AND SOUR PEPPER JAM

This is one of the most popular and best-selling of the relishes I make. It is good on hamburgers and, mixed with cream cheese, makes an excellent spread for crackers. One customer tells me that a half-pint bottle is just right for glazing a rack of spareribs.

> 12 *large peppers—preferably red*
> 1 *tbsp. salt*
> 2 *cups sugar*
> 2 *cups vinegar*

Put the peppers through the fine disk of the food mill. Sprinkle the peppers with the salt and let stand 3 hours. Pour the pulp into a fine sieve and run cold water through it to remove some of the salt. Put the pulp into a saucepan; add sugar and vinegar and bring to a boil, stirring constantly until you are sure all sugar is dissolved. Reduce heat and simmer until the jam gets quite thick. Pour into hot, sterilized jars and seal.

Yield: 2-1/2 pints.

HELEN'S CUCUMBER RELISH

This has a crisp, fresh taste that sets it apart from other relishes.

> 6 *qts. cucumbers, ends removed but not peeled*
> 1 *qt. medium onions*

1 *cup salt*
9 *cups cold water*
6 *cups sugar*
5 *cups vinegar*
1/2 *tbsp. turmeric*
1 *tsp. mustard seed*
1 *tsp. celery seed*

Put cucumbers and onions through the medium blade of the food mill. Mix with the salt in a bowl and cover with the water. Let stand 3 hours. Drain. Boil the sugar and vinegar to make a syrup. Add the vegetables and spices and simmer until the vegetables are tender. Ladle into hot, sterilized jars and seal.

Yield: About 7 pints.

SPICED CHERRY RELISH

This is a good garnish for fowl—especially duck—and is a good base for an unusual sweet-and-sour barbecue sauce.

6 *cups sweet cherries, stemmed and stoned*
white vinegar to cover
6 *cups sugar* or *honey*

Put the cherries in a bowl or small crock and cover with the vinegar. Let stand 7 days. Keep all cherries submerged by weighing down with a plate. Drain on the 7th day. Wash the crock and arrange the cherries in it, mixing in the sugar at the same time. Cover the crock and let the cherries stand for 7 days. Stir them gently once a day. Remove the cherries with a slotted spoon and pack them in sterilized jars. Heat the juice and sugar in the crock until it forms a light syrup. Pour the hot syrup over the cherries to within 1/2 inch of the top of the jar, and seal.

Yield: About 2-1/2 pints.

TOMATO KETCHUP

Make this with dead ripe tomatoes that may otherwise go to waste. Three batches a summer will provide enough for the table, for use in barbecue sauces and for sending an occasional bottle home with an appreciative guest. Do not double the recipe; a larger amount may necessitate a longer cooking time and may result in darker color and flavor.

> 10 lbs. red tomatoes
> 5 sweet red peppers
> 5 onions
> 3-1/2 cups vinegar
> 3-1/2 cups sugar
> 3 tbsp. salt
> 4 tsp. dry mustard
> 2 tsp. allspice
> 2 tsp. cloves
> 2 tsp. cinnamon
> 1 tsp. hot red pepper

Remove the stem ends of the tomatoes and seed the peppers. Peel the onions. Cut the vegetables into chunks and purée them in the blender. Pour purée in a heavy-bottomed kettle. Add the vinegar, sugar, salt and mustard. Tie allspice, cloves, cinnamon and hot pepper in a cheesecloth bag and add to ketchup. Simmer, stirring frequently, until thick. (If you don't have time to stir frequently, put the purée in a large roasting pan and simmer it on the middle rack of a 300° oven.) Remove spice bag; pour hot ketchup into hot, sterilized jars, and seal.

Yield varies according to water content of tomatoes: 5 to 7 pints.

FRUIT KETCHUP

This is delicious and different. Do make it at least once.

15 large ripe tomatoes, peeled and seeded
3 onions, peeled
3 peaches, stoned and peeled
3 pears, cored and skinned
2 green peppers, seeded
1 cup chopped celery
2 cups sugar
2 cups vinegar
1 tbsp. salt
1 1-oz. box whole pickling spices, tied in cheesecloth

Mince all vegetables and fruit or whirl briefly in the blender. Pour into heavy kettle; add sugar, vinegar and spices and simmer 2 hours, stirring frequently. Remove spice bag. Pour ketchup into hot, sterilized jars and seal.

Yield: 6 to 8 pints.

FRESH RELISHES

NORFOLK RELISH

All the ingredients of this raw relish are usually on hand year round, so you can make it in summer as a chill accompaniment to cold meats or as a fresh winter garnish for meatloaf and pot roast.

2 cups celery
2 cups apples, cored but not peeled
2 cups onions, peeled
1/2 cup vinegar
1/2 cup salad oil
salt and pepper to taste

Put celery, apples and onions through the medium blade of the food mill. Combine with vinegar, oil and seasonings. Chill for at least 2 hours, stirring thoroughly every half hour. This recipe makes 1-1/2 quarts of relish—enough for two generous bowls on a table set for 10. Leftovers can be made into barbecue sauce.

PURI'S RELISH

This is a westernized version of an Indian friend's approximation of a relish made by his cook in Bangalore. It goes well with cold roast beef and pork.

> 2 *whole dried red chili peppers*
> 2 *apples, cored but not pared*
> 2 *medium onions, peeled*
> 1 *orange*
> *bourbon or whiskey*

Put the peppers, apples, onions and entire orange through the medium blade of the food mill. Moisten the relish with bourbon or a good blended whiskey; chill and serve. This yields about 1-1/2 cups relish—enough to serve 4 to 6 people.

SALSA CRUDA (RAW SAUCE)

Put a bowl of this on the table and let the diners put it on what they will—hot dogs, hamburgers, rice, zucchini and all meats. This sauce, thinned with tomato purée, dressed the most memorable shrimp cocktail I ever ate.

> 2 *large ripe tomatoes, skinned and seeded*
> 1 *clove garlic*
> 2 *fresh red chili peppers*
> *juice of 1 lime* or *2 tbsp. vinegar*
> 1 *tsp. salt*

Whirl tomatoes, garlic and chilis in blender briefly, or dice fine and then mash together well in a bowl. Add lime juice and salt; stir well. Serve at room temperature with omelets, rice or bean dishes.

Yield: About 1 cup.

CHUTNIES

The growing popularity of curried dishes has led to an increased acceptance of chutney. Imported chutnies made with tamarind and mango are very good, but quite expensive. Most of these homemade chutnies are economical and unusual. Chutnies go well with meats, fowl and game, as well as the traditional curries.

Four of these recipes call for fresh ginger root, which can be bought in Chinese and West Indian grocery stores. Dried ginger root, soaked in water for several hours, can be substituted.

APPLE CHUTNEY

1 lb. brown sugar
2 cups cider vinegar
2 tbsp. mustard seed
3 tbsp. minced ginger root
1 tsp. ground cloves
1/2 tsp. cayenne pepper
1 tsp. salt
1 lemon, seeded but not peeled, chopped
1 cup raisins
1 cup green pepper, chopped
1 cup onion, chopped
5 cups apples, cored but not peeled

Combine the sugar, vinegar and spices in a large saucepan and bring slowly to a boil, stirring until sugar is dissolved. Add the remaining ingredients; reduce heat and simmer until the chutney thickens—usually about 45 minutes. Ladle into hot, sterilized jars and seal.

Yield: About 3 pints.

WINTER CHUTNEY

2 *cups brown sugar*
1 *tbsp. curry powder*
1 *tsp. each cinnamon, clove, allspice, ground black pepper*
1/4 *cup scraped ginger root*
grated rind and juice of 2 lemons
2 *cups vinegar*
1 *lb. dried figs or currants*
1 *lb. pitted dates*
1 *lb. dried apricots, pitted, soaked in water and drained*
1 *lb. prunes, pitted, soaked and drained*
12 *apples, cored and chopped*
3 *medium onions, diced*
vinegar
1/2 *cup sherry*

Combine sugar, spices, lemon rind and juice, and the 2 cups vinegar in a large saucepan and bring to a boil. Reduce heat; add fruit and onions. Stir well and add enough vinegar to cover fruit. Simmer until chutney thickens—usually about 2 hours. Stir in sherry. Let the chutney cool to lukewarm. Pack in sterilized, hot jars and seal.

Yield: 10–12 pints.

GREEN TOMATO CHUTNEY

3 *tbsp. salt*
12 *large green tomatoes, seeded and chopped*
12 *tart apples, cored, peeled and chopped*
2 *green peppers, chopped*

2-1/2 cups raisins
4 cups vinegar
4 cups brown sugar
1 cup lemon juice
3 tbsp. mustard seed
2 tbsp. fresh ginger root, minced
1 tsp. paprika

Sprinkle the salt over the green tomatoes and let stand overnight. Drain. In a stainless steel or enameled kettle, combine tomatoes with the apples, peppers, raisins and vinegar. Simmer 2 hours. Add the remaining ingredients and simmer until slightly thickened—about 1 hour. Pack in hot, sterilized jars and seal.

Yield: About 7 pints.

PLUM CHUTNEY

1 qt. cider vinegar
2 cups sugar
1 tbsp. salt
1 tsp. ground cloves
1 tsp. ground allspice
2 tbsp. ginger root, minced
1 lb. raisins
3 apples, cored, pared and coarsely chopped
2 medium onions, diced fine
20 plums, pitted and coarsely chopped

Combine vinegar, sugar and spices in a stainless steel or enameled saucepan and bring to a boil, stirring to be sure that all the sugar is dissolved. Add raisins, apples and onions and cook over a medium heat until apples and onions are just tender. Add plums and simmer until chutney thickens. Ladle into hot, sterilized jars and seal.

Yield: About 4 pints.

PEAR CHUTNEY

Kieffer pears, too gritty for eating out of hand, are very good for chutney.

5 lbs. pears, pared, cored and coarsely chopped
1 cup water
1-1/2 lbs. light brown sugar
1 lb. yellow raisins
2 tbsp. mustard seed
1 tbsp. salt
2 tbsp. dry red pepper, crushed
1/4 cup scraped ginger root
1 qt. white vinegar

Combine pears, water and sugar in a large saucepan and cook over a very low heat, stirring constantly to prevent scorching, until sugar dissolves. The mixture will thicken very quickly. Add the remaining ingredients; stir well and bring to a boil. Remove from heat. Cover the saucepan and let the chutney sit for 10 hours or overnight at room temperature. Next day, bring mixture to a boil, then reduce heat and simmer until the chutney thickens—usually 45 minutes to 1 hour—stirring frequently. Pour into hot, sterilized jars and seal.

Yield: About 5 pints.

HOMEMADE SPICE BLENDS

A roommate from India introduced me to curry, for which she concocted her own curry powders. I have been making my own ever since. I grind spices in a tabletop corn mill. A coffee grinder is fine. For small amounts, use a mortar and pestle. Feel free to experiment with the proportions of spices to suit your own taste. The coarser texture of the home-ground spices and their freshness make superior curried dishes. Four- or six-ounce jars of curry powder and the other spice blends given here make nice gifts and unusual items for bazaars. Make only as much curry powder as you will use, give away or sell in one month's time.

Cardamom seeds have to be skinned—use only the seeds inside the brown or green pods. It is a tedious job—do it while talking on the phone or listening to the news. It is possible, with practice, to skin cardamom and read at the same time.

If a curry powder turns out to be harsh, the flavor can be softened by the addition of a good pinch of fresh grated orange or lemon peel at cooking time.

You can enliven and vary curries by using fresh herbs in season. Parsley, thyme, rosemary, anise and dill—very finely chopped—all go well with curry.

CURRY POWDER

8 *tbsp. each coriander, turmeric, cumin*
4 *tbsp. each black peppercorns, ground dry ginger*
2 *tbsp. each fenugreek, cardamom, chili powder*
1 *tbsp. each mustard seed, clove, poppy seed*

Grind the coriander, cumin, pepper, cardamom, mustard, clove and poppy seeds. If you do not have a grinder, use ground clove, since whole cloves are very hard to grind in a mortar and pestle. Combine with the already ground spices (turmeric, ginger, etc.) and mix thoroughly. Store in jars with tight-fitting lids and keep in a cool, dark place.

MADRAS CURRY POWDER

This has a lighter flavor than the preceding formula—the coriander and cardamom dominate.

4 *tbsp. coriander*
seed of 30 cardamoms
5 *tsp. turmeric*
3 *tsp. cumin*
2 *tsp. each black peppercorns, fenugreek, mace*
1 *tsp. dry ginger, ground*
1-1/2 *tbsp. each poppy seed, mustard seed*
1/2 *tsp. each clove, garlic powder*

Grind whole spices. Combine all ingredients, mix well and store in airtight jars in a cool, dark place.

GARAM MASALA

Use this instead of curry powder to make a sweet curried rice (p. 67) for people who do not like hot curry. A pinch of garam masala in oatmeal cookie dough or rice pudding gives a delicate spiciness.

1 *tbsp. each black peppercorns, black caraway seeds*
3 *tbsp. coriander*
1/2 *tsp. each ground clove, cinnamon*
20 to 30 *cardamom seeds*

Grind the whole spices. Mix all spices together and store in an airtight container in a cool, dark place.

CHATAAR

Sprinkle this simple spice blend on fish before broiling, or add a pinch to the flour used for dredging chicken. Chataar also makes a good and unusual dip. Dunk bread, crackers or bread sticks into a bowl of hot olive oil or melted butter, then into chataar. Double this recipe to make a bowl of dip.

6 *tbsp. sesame seeds*
6 *tsp. dried thyme, crumbled*

3 *tsp. imported powder sumac (sometimes called Aleppo sumac)*

Toast the sesame seeds until they are golden brown. Mix well with the thyme and sumac. Use immediately or refrigerate in an airtight container.

QUATRE ÉPICES (FOUR SPICES)

Use this to season pork in any form and to make a difference in scalloped potatoes (p. 93).

7 *tbsp. black peppercorns*
1 *tbsp. nutmeg, grated or ground*
1 *tbsp. ground clove*
1 *tbsp. ground cinnamon*

Crush peppercorns in mortar and mix with the other spices. Store in an airtight jar. This keeps well for several months.

SWEET PRESERVES AND SPREADS

If you want to grow some of your own tree fruits to provide the basic ingredients for preserves, by all means plant a crab-apple tree and some quince and peach trees. These fruit trees come into bearing early and are generally prolific. With rhubarb, strawberries and grapes from the garden, it is easy and inexpensive to stock the larder with a variety of jellies, jams and preserves.

Do use a candy or jelly thermometer to take the guesswork out of jelly-making.

A device that every serious jelly-maker should know about is the Jelmeter, used to determine the proper amount of sugar for each batch of juice for jelly. It is a viscosity pipette available from, of all places, the Delaware Motor Sales Co., Wilmington, Delaware. The tube is filled with the juice to be used for jelly. The juice is permitted to flow from the tube for exactly 60 seconds. The level of juice remaining in the tube shows the amount of sugar to be used for each cup of juice.

APPLE JELLY WITH ROSE GERANIUM

This is a standard recipe for apple jelly. I include it in the hope that you will try it. The rose geranium leaf gives a lovely faint rose flavor that turns prosaic apple jelly into something special. There are a number of varieties of rose-scented geraniums—attar of roses, old-fashioned rose or cinnamon rose are the best to flavor jelly.

> *9 apples, tart and hard*
> *water to cover*
> *sugar as needed*
> *rose geranium leaves*

Cut out the blossom and stem end of the apples and slice them. Put apples in a kettle with just enough water to cover. Bring to a boil, then simmer until the fruit is quite soft. Pour the contents of the kettle into a muslin bag and suspend the bag over a saucepan. Let the liquid drain. Do not squeeze the bag, or some of the pulp may be forced out and the jelly will not be clear. Measure the liquid; add 3/4 cup sugar to each cup of juice and stir to dissolve. Boil until the jelly thermometer registers 222°. Skim any scum from the surface. Bruise slightly small pieces of rose geranium leaf and put a piece in each jar. Pour the hot jelly into the jars. The pieces of leaf will slowly rise to the surface. Lift the leaves out with the tip of a knife blade. Seal the jars and let cool.

Yield: About 2 pints.

CRABAPPLE JELLY

Perfect with cornbread and cornmeal muffins.

15 crabapples
8 cups water
sugar as needed

Remove the stem and blossom end from crabapples, and cut into quarters. Place them in a kettle with the water and bring to a boil. Reduce the heat and simmer until the crabapples are *very* soft. Pour the apples and juice into a muslin jelly bag suspended over a saucepan, and let drain. Do not try to force the liquid from the bag by hand, or jelly may be cloudy. Measure the juice and add 3/4 cup sugar for every cup of juice. Stir to dissolve sugar; bring to a boil and cook until the jelly thermometer registers 222°. Skim any scum from the surface. Pour hot jelly into hot, sterilized jars and seal.

Yield: About 2-1/2 pints.

GRAPE JAM

When grape vines begin to bear, you soon find you have more grapes than you can eat out of hand, but not enough to make wine. Make grape jam—it's easy, delicious and fool-proof. You can squeeze the pulp from the skins of 2 lbs. of grapes while 3-minute eggs are cooking.

3 lbs. stemmed Concord-type purple grapes
water to cover
sugar as needed

Squeeze each grape so that the pulp is forced from the skin. Collect the pulp in one saucepan and put the skins in another. Chop the skins coarsely in the pan so as not to lose any juice—a double-bladed pastry blender works well. Add just enough water to the skins to prevent scorching, and cook for 20 minutes. Cook the pulp in its pan until soft—about 5 minutes—and then press through a sieve fine enough to retain the seeds. Add the strained pulp to the cooked skins. Measure and add 3 cups sugar to each quart of fruit. Bring to a boil and cook rapidly, stirring constantly, until thermometer registers 222°. Pour into hot, sterilized jars and seal.

Yield: About 2 pints.

SPICED PEARS

These are nice to have on hand for a change from juice at breakfast, to add to fruit cup, or to serve alone as a light dessert.

> 4 *lbs. very firm pears*
> 1 *cup water*
> *juice and rind of 1 lemon*
> 1 *1-inch piece ginger root, scrubbed and bruised*

Peel, core and cut the pears into 1/2-inch-thick slices. Put the water and lemon juice into a large saucepan. Cut the lemon peel into thin strips. Add lemon rind, sugar and ginger to the water and simmer, stirring to be sure sugar dissolves, until the mixture forms a syrup—about 15 minutes. Add the pear slices and simmer until pears become transparent. Ladle pears into hot, sterilized jars; fill with the hot syrup to within 1/2 inch of the top, and seal.

Yield: About 3-1/2 pints.

Quince trees are small, compact, ornamental and relatively carefree. If you like to put up your own preserves, by all means plant a few quince trees. They come into bearing early; only strawberries and grapes will give a quicker return.

QUINCE HONEY

This is delicious on French toast, pancakes, waffles and ice cream.

6 *medium quinces*
4 *cups sugar*
1 *tbsp. lemon juice*
3 *cups water*

Core the quinces and cut out any spots or wasp bites, but do not peel. Put quinces through the fine blade of the food mill. For a finer texture, blend the quinces at high speed until smooth. Put quince pulp, sugar, lemon juice and water into a stainless steel or enameled pan and cook until slightly thickened. When cooked, the quince honey will be a tawny orange-red color. Ladle into hot jars and seal.

Yield: 3 to 4 pints.

QUINCE JELLY

This is very easy to make, since the quinces need only to be washed and chopped. Use as many quinces as you like or have on hand.

Cut quinces into small chunks and cook in water to cover until very tender. Strain the juice through a muslin jelly bag. Measure and add 1 cup sugar to each cup of juice. Boil to jellying point and pour into sterilized jars or jelly glasses. Let cool until jelly begins to set before sealing.

QUINCE MARMALADE

6 *quinces*
3 *apples*
sugar as needed

Core, peel and chop quinces and apples. Cook quinces in water to cover until tender. Add apple chunks and cook an additional 7 to 10 minutes—until apples are tender. Measure the fruit and juice and add 3/4 cup sugar for each cup of marmalade. Boil to jellying point. Pour into hot, sterilized jars; let cool to lukewarm, and seal.

Yield: About 3-1/2 pints.

The first frost warning of autumn always arrives too soon. Here are three ways to keep the last of the tomato crop from going to waste.

GREEN TOMATO MINCEMEAT

This recipe contains no suet or meat and keeps well in mason jars. One quart fills a 9-inch pie shell.

24 *medium green tomatoes, cored and chopped*
10 *medium apples, cored, pared and chopped*
1 *lb. raisins*
1 *tbsp. cinnamon*
2 *tsp. salt*
1/2 *tsp. ground allspice*
3 *cups brown sugar*
2 *cups white sugar*
1 *cup vinegar*
2 *cups water*

Combine all ingredients and cook over low heat, stirring frequently, about 1 hour, or until apple chunks are tender and mixture has begun to thicken. Pour into hot, sterilized jars and seal at once.

Yield: 3 quarts.

TOMATO PRESERVES

2 *lbs. red or yellow tomatoes*
2 *cups sugar*
1 *lemon*

Cover the tomatoes with boiling water and let stand 2 minutes. Drain and peel tomatoes carefully, keeping them whole. Place the tomatoes in layers sprinkled with the sugar in a bowl or enamel kettle, and let stand overnight. Drain and cook the juice to the jellying point. Add thinly sliced lemon and the tomatoes. Cook until clear and thick. Seal in hot, sterilized jars.

Yield: 2 pints.

TOMATO MARMALADE

1 qt. *ripe tomatoes*
2 *oranges*
1 *lemon*
2 *lbs. sugar*

Peel tomatoes and measure 1 quart firmly packed. Simmer tomatoes in a heavy saucepan. Add the pulp of the oranges and lemon when the tomatoes begin to boil. Cut the orange and lemon peel into narrow strips and add to the mixture. Add sugar and stir until fruit peel becomes transparent. Pour into hot jars; cool and seal.

Yield: 3 pints.

BERRY SYRUP AND PURÉE

Extend the pleasures of the brief berry season with berry syrups and purées to serve with pancakes and waffles, in milkshakes, desserts and punches.

BLACKBERRY SYRUP

6 *qts. blackberries*
2-1/2 *qts. water*
sugar as needed

Wash, stem and crush the berries. Combine with water and boil rapidly for 10 minutes. Reduce the heat and simmer for 5 minutes. Strain the juice through a jelly bag. For each 6 cups of juice, add 4 cups sugar. Boil until slightly thickened. Pour hot syrup into hot, sterilized jars and seal. Store away from bright light.

Yield: Varies greatly depending on berries—generally 6–8 pints.

RASPBERRY PURÉE

 1 qt. raspberries
 2 cups sugar
 1/8 tsp. cream of tartar
 1/2 cup water

Mash the berries through a fine sieve. Combine sugar, cream of tartar and water in a small saucepan. Cover and bring to a boil. Uncover and let boil briskly until the syrup will spin a short thread. Combine the syrup and raspberry pulp. Use at once or freeze in 1/2-pint containers.

Yield: 2 half-pints.

RASPBERRY VINEGAR

This makes a difference in your salads.

 2 qts. raspberries (or blackberries)
 1 qt. cider vinegar
 sugar as needed

Do not wash berries but remove the stems. Put berries in a bowl, crush them slightly, and add the vinegar. Cover and let stand at room temperature for 24 hours. Strain the vinegar through several layers of cheesecloth. Add 1 cup sugar to each quart of vinegar. Simmer for 20 minutes, skimming any scum that rises to the surface. Pour liquid into hot, sterilized jars and store in a cool, dark place.

DRIED VEGETABLES AND FRUIT

As energy costs rise, excessive use of stoves and freezers disturb the domestic economy. Many vegetables can be stored in their natural state: potatoes, onions, carrots, cabbage, winter squash and turnips keep well in cold cellars or pits. Brussels sprouts, parsnips and salsify can be harvested directly from the garden through mid-winter. The flavor of all three is felt by many to be improved by frost.

Some fruits and vegetables can be dried at home. Modern experts advise gas or electric heat driers, and color fixing by the use of sulfur fumes. My grandmother dried her currants and corn, beans and peas, apples and plums in shallow tin trays set out on a tin-covered porch roof or the concrete cap of a big well, without benefit of chemistry or thermostats.

Apples, currants and *plums* should be picked when fully ripe. Core and slice apples and spread on trays. Put the trays in the sun, preferably on a surface that will reflect dry heat. Bring the trays in at sunset; put them out when the sun is well risen. Three or four days of strong sun will usually dry the apples sufficiently, so that they are pliable but no longer wet in the center. String the slices and hang them in a dry place or store them in shallow wooden trays and turn the slices over from time to time.

Currants can be dried whole.

Plums should be halved and pitted, and dried with the cut side toward the sun. Not all plums are prunes, although all prunes are plums. The varieties that will dry without fermenting while still in possession of their pits are prunes.

Dried apples, currants and plums will be useful in pies and puddings. They will also help stretch the expensive dried fruits (citron, cherries, etc.) needed for fruitcake.

The best sweet *corn* for drying is the sweet white type called shoepeg—the best-known variety is Country Gentleman. Whether you grow your own shoepeg or buy golden bantam, you can dry it. If possible, use corn just picked and not quite fully ripe. Strip the husks back, remove the silk, and hang the ears by the husks in a dry shady place. When the kernels are dry, you can hang the husks from an attic rafter and shell as needed. Or shell the corn at once and store in muslin bags hung in a dry place.

SCHNITZ UND KNEPP

This Pennsylvania Dutch dish is a perfect one-dish lunch for cold winter days. *Schnitz* means a section of dried fruit, *Knepp* are dumplings.

> 2 *cups dried apple slices*
> *water*
> 2 *lbs. smoked pork—shoulder, ham, hocks, etc.*
> 2 *tbsp. sugar*
> 1 *tsp. salt*

Soak apples overnight in water to cover, adding more water when needed to keep fruit covered. Boil the smoked pork until it is tender. Combine the pork and apples in a large skillet or kettle that has a close-fitting lid. Add the water that the apples were soaking in, the sugar and the salt, and simmer until the apples are tender. While the kettle is simmering, make the dumplings.

DUMPLINGS

> 1 *cup flour*
> 1 *tsp. baking powder*
> *pinch of salt*
> 1 *egg*
> *cold water as needed*

Sift together the flour, baking powder and salt. Beat the egg and add it to the dry ingredients along with just enough cold water to make a thick batter.

Drop spoonfuls of the batter among the apples. Cover tightly and let boil gently 10 minutes without lifting the lid. Serve at once.

CHAPTER 6

House and Garden

V ISITORS viewing the herb garden and the homemade concoctions for house and garden that come from it often say, "I'd love to do all this—if I only had the time." But at least half the drawback is lack of space. Gardens, pantries and potting sheds require room, as do the kettles and tubs for making soap and newspaper logs. I have lots of pantry space, a workroom, and out-of-the-way spots where I can let lard, ashes, newspapers, etc. accumulate until needed.

HERBS

If you get the herb garden urge, remember that all gardens must be weeded and watered. If your main interest is in annual kitchen herbs, you can grow most of them among the flowers and vegetables of the main gardens. However, if you also want to make potpourris, herbal moth repellants and pillows, you will need space in an herb garden or among perennial flowers for perennial herbs. I grow 39 herbs, 22 of which are perennials. All but lavender grow in a plot 15 feet by 24 feet. In this space I also grow most of the annual herbs and some early radishes, lettuce and scallions.

If you are growing herbs for the first time, take care not to grow too many of each kind. You usually need only a few leaves from each at any given time.

PERENNIALS

Of 21 kitchen herbs I use, 13 are perennials. If you decide to grow any of these, put them where they will not be destroyed by plough or lawnmower.

Burnet. Few people in my area seem to know burnet. If you can't find plants for sale, order seed from a reputable seed house. You will have leaves for use the following spring. The tender top leaves give a cucumber flavor to early spring salads. Burnet will do well in partial shade or in a spot that gets morning sun only. One or two plants are plenty. Burnet grows in neat round clumps and will stay trim looking if flower heads are removed as they begin to emerge. Burnet does not dry well and the plants do not thrive over winter indoors.

BURNET VINEGAR

1 qt. white vinegar
1 qt. dry white wine
2 cups burnet leaves, chopped

Simmer all three ingredients on a very low flame for 15 minutes. Pour into sterilized bottles, put a fresh sprig of burnet in each and cork tightly.

Chives. You can buy well grown chives in pots at plant centers or supermarkets. If you grow chives from seed, they will be very spindly the first year. Chives give a delicate onion flavor and specks of green color to sauces, soups, stews and, of course, the sour cream dressing for baked potatoes.

Chives dry well. Cut them in the morning when the dew has dried. Line a baking pan with paper towels, chop the chives into the pan and dry in a 150° oven. Store in airtight containers out of bright light until needed.

I bought "garlic chive" seeds a number of years ago at the Philadelphia Flower Show. I have been unable to identify garlic chive in the garden encyclopedia. It's very useful in summer when the winter supply of garlic cloves has been used up.

Lemon balm. One plant is enough. Buy one or get a slip from a friend. Keep lemon balm trimmed into a low round form, or it will sprawl and spread. Use balm to flavor iced tea and orangeade. cucumber salads and tarragon vinegar. Hens like lemon balm. Throw them the trimmings from the bush, or grow some balm just outside their run so they can pick at it but not kill it.

Lovage is easily grown from seed or root division. One plant will make a clump by the second season. The leaves give a celery flavor to stews and soups but should be used sparingly as they are *very* strongly flavored. Since I grow celery and celeriac now, I no longer use lovage.

Mints. Orange mint, spearmint and peppermint are winter hardy. All three make good herbal teas which require no sweetening. Spearmint and orange mint are good in iced tea and lemonade. Mints are great ramblers. To keep them confined, plant them inside a sunken piece of ceramic pipe or barrel or an old bucket that has begun to leak. (To get the most use from a bucket, use it in the house or barn when it is new. After it begins to corrode, demote it to the greenhouse. When it begins to leak, use it as the scraping board bucket in the henhouse. When the holes in the bottom become too large for even this job, sink it in the garden to confine the roots of invasive plants.)

Oregano survives winter in my herb garden since I planted it in the most sheltered, best drained part of the plot. Fresh oregano is not so piquant as dried. Use fresh chopped leaves on sliced tomatoes, in green salads and, fresh or dried, in soups, stews and sauces.

Rosemary grows next to the oregano—it will not survive even a fairly mild winter if its roots are in soggy soil. Rosemary is a perfect seasoning for chicken, veal and lamb. Use portions of branches in baked loin of pork and lamb. Remove the branch after baking and you will have the flavoring without the annoyance of the leaves, which are rather woody in texture. Rosemary has an ancient reputation as a moth chaser and, bruised, is effective in potpourri.

ROSEMARY SAUTERNE JELLY

1/2 cup boiling water
3 tbsp. fresh rosemary leaves
1-1/2 cups sauterne or other dry white wine
1/8 tsp. salt
1 bay leaf
2 cups sugar
few drops of yellow or orange food coloring
1/2 cup fruit pectin

Pour the boiling water over the rosemary leaves and let steep 15 minutes. Strain through several layers of cheesecloth and add enough water to make 1/2 cup. Pour rosemary water into an enameled or stainless steel pan; add wine, salt and bay leaf. Stir in the sugar and gradually bring the mixture to a boil. Add food coloring and fruit pectin. Stir constantly and allow to boil briskly for 1 full minute. Remove from heat at once and skim. Pour into hot, sterilized jars and seal. This jelly is good on dark muffins—whole wheat, bran or rye—and goes well with venison.

Yield: 1 pint.

ROSEMARY LEMONADE

1 cup sugar
4 cups water
2/3 cup lemon juice
1 tsp. rosemary leaves, dry or 1 tbsp. fresh leaves
pinch of salt
fresh lemon slices

Combine sugar, water and 1 tbsp. lemon juice in saucepan. Add rosemary and salt; mix well and bring to a boil. Remove from heat and let steep 5 minutes. Strain out the rosemary leaves. Cool the liquid and add to remaining water and lemon juice. Serve in tall glasses filled with cracked ice and garnish with lemon slices.

Yield: 1 pitcher full—serves 4 generously.

FOUR THIEVES VINEGAR

1/4 cup fresh rosemary leaves (1/8 cup dry leaves)
3/4 cup fresh mint (3 tbsp. dry leaves)
2 tbsp. fresh sage (1 tbsp. dry leaves)
1/2 tsp. black pepper
5 or 6 whole cloves

1 *piece stick cinnamon about 1 inch long*
3 *bay leaves*
2 *tsp. salt*
2 *qts. red wine vinegar*
whole cloves of garlic

Put all ingredients except garlic into a small crock or earthen-ware jug. Cover tightly with paper and let stand 2 weeks. Stir occasionally. Strain the vinegar through several layers of wet cheesecloth into sterilized bottles. Put a whole clove of garlic into each bottle and cork tightly. Store away from light and heat, until given as a gift or used in salads and marinades.

Yield: 2 quarts.

Sage. One plant will soon become a neat round bush if you keep it trimmed, and will supply your needs, fresh in summer, dried in winter.

Tarragon grows in full sun or partial shade. Start it from root divisions and keep the clump compact. Tarragon is useful in sauces for fish and chicken, salad dressings and herb vinegars.

Thyme is an excellent edging plant and is a good subject for the dry, sunny rock garden. Creeping thyme is a good ground cover. All varieties are good for seasoning and attractive to bees. Some of the fancy thymes—lemon thyme, silver edged, etc.—are not winter hardy in the northern parts of the U.S.

ANNUALS

There are eight annual kitchen herbs in the garden. I include biennial parsley in this list because I treat it as an annual.

Basil is easily grown from seed. Donate extra plants to June hospital fêtes or church bazaars. Some of my neighbors keep basil in pots and window boxes through the summer to keep away flies and mosquitoes.

BASIL VINEGAR

Steep a handful of fresh leaves or 2 tbsp. dried leaves in 1 quart vinegar for 10 minutes. Strain and bottle.

Chervil is used much as parsley in cooking. Sow it when you sow parsley in early spring. I find it does best in partial shade.

Coriander, one of the oldest seasonings known to man, is not well known in this country. It is a very tender annual. Sow it when the ground has warmed thoroughly. Use the leaves in salad dressings and sauces for fish. Do *not* use the coriander seeds when they are green. The smell alone should deter you. Dry the seeds in the sun or in a very slow oven, and use to season pickled beets and curries.

Dill grows easily and rapidly from seed. Since it is frail and apt to be laid low by the wind, I find it best to grow dill in a square patch, surrounded by 3-foot poles (broom handles will do), with twine as fence going around and through the dill plants.

Marjoram plants can be bought in spring at many plant centers. One plant is enough. If you repot the new plant in a slightly larger pot and plunge the pot in the garden, the plant can be lifted and brought indoors to winter over.

Nasturtium. Low growing dwarf nasturtiums make a good front border for flower beds; tall climbing varieties are best trained on fences and trellises. A sandy lean soil is best. If the ground is too rich, the plant will produce luxuriant vines but few flowers. Young nasturtium leaves taste like watercress and can be used in salads. The young unopened flower buds can be pickled and used as capers.

NASTURTIUM SEED CAPERS

2 *cups nasturtium flower pods*
1 *cup distilled white vinegar*
1 *tbsp. salt*

Pack the buds in a clean bottle. Dissolve the salt in the vinegar, pour over the capers to 1/4 inch of the top and seal. Store in a cool, dark place 6 weeks before using.

Summer savory, like coriander, is too little used. Grow it from seed and plant a patch of 6 to 12 plants in a sunny spot. Use fresh savory rather generously in salads and in stews and soups.

Rose geranium leaves give a novel and old-fashioned flavor to apple jelly and pound cake. Most varieties of rose geranium make fairly large bushes by the end of summer, so allow plenty of room around the new plant. Use leaves in potpourri and linen closets. Root a cutting at the end of autumn, and winter it over indoors to provide next year's plant.

Besides the kitchen herbs, I grow *bergamot* and *borage*—mainly for the bees—*chamomile* for tea, *germander* and *santolina* for edging plants, *hyssop* and *pennyroyal* for insect repellants, *lavender* for sachet. *Southernwood, wormwood* and *camphor-scented southernwood* clippings are strewn in the henhouse to discourage bugs. Southernwood foliage steeped in hot water makes a good shampoo. The foliage of all the *artemisias* can be used as fillers in flower arrangements and herbal wreaths. Put wormwood clippings, hyssop and rue beneath doormats in summer to discourage ants.

FOR THE HOUSE AND GARDEN AND JUST FOR FUN

I first became interested in homemade soaps, potpourri, etc. through a nostalgia for the old-fashioned way of life. However, as prices rise and as warnings multiply regarding common household products from aerosol containers to soaps that may be too efficient, the appeal of homemade preparations for the house and garden and personal use grows apace.

HOMEMADE SOAP

You can use bacon fat, drippings and fat trimmings from meat. Strain the drippings as you get them into a can until soap-making time.

> 3 *pts. water*
> 1 *can lye*
> 1/2 *cup kerosene*
> 1/2 *cup ammonia*
> 4 *tbsp. borax*
> 5 *lbs. grease*

Combine all ingredients except grease in a large enamel basin or lard tin. Do not use an aluminum container. Stir with a wooden paddle and let cool.

Melt the grease in 1 quart water. Clean grease will float to the top. Lift it off and add it to the lye mixture. Stir well. When it begins to thicken, pour the soap into loaf pans that have been lined with old muslin or cotton cloth. Cut the soap into cakes after a few hours. If it is allowed to harden completely, the soap will shatter when you try to cut it.

WHITEWASH

Use this for the interiors of henhouses, barns, cellars, potting sheds, etc.

5 *lbs. hydrated lime*
boiling water
1 *lb. rock salt*
1 *lb. alum*

Slake the lime in the boiling water until it cools. Stir in rock salt and alum until they are dissolved. Apply to walls with a broad whitewash brush.

POTPOURRI

Dried rose petals form the base of this potpourri. Gather the petals after the dew has dried. Spread the petals on an old sheet and let them dry 4 or 5 days in a cool dark place—perhaps an attic room. Put the dried petals in a bowl, alternating layers of petals with layers of salt. Cover the bowl and let it sit 10 days. Mix in crushed orris root, if you have it, and then add scents to suit your fancy. Calamus root, cedar chips, lavender, orangemint, orange peel, rose geranium leaves, rosemary and verbena are ingredients that you may very well have on hand or can buy. The southernwoods, hyssop, pennyroyal and goosefoot add sharp pungent accents that do not appeal to everyone.

FURNITURE POLISH

This is very good to use on wood that has been recently refinished. Simply mix equal parts of turpentine, linseed oil and cider vinegar. Rub the wood well with it and let stand overnight. Rub well with a clean cloth before waxing.

SUNTAN LOTION

Mix two parts olive oil with one part vinegar. This works well on people who tan nicely, but it won't do a thing for redheads or others who are sensitive to the sun.

NEWSPAPER LOGS FOR COLORFUL FIRES

These logs will provide brightly colored flames in a fireplace for at least an hour. They are nice to give to friends or to sell at bazaars. You need two months' preparation and stone tubs to soak them in. The copper sulphate and rock salt will erode metal tubs badly. Stone tubs are often offered at country sales.

To make 5 logs:

>   *150 sheets newspaper*
>   *4 lbs. blue stone crystals (available at farm supply stores)*
>   *4 lbs. copper sulphate*
>   *3 lbs. rock salt*
>   *1-1/2 gal. water*

Roll 30 sheets of paper tightly into a roll, and tie firmly around each end and in the center with very stout string. Mix the chemicals in a tub with the water. Add the logs. Let the logs soak for 4 weeks, adding water when necessary to keep moist. At the end of the 4th week, remove the logs. Let dry for one month before using. Gift logs should be wrapped with a single sheet of gift-wrapping paper—preferably unglazed.

INK FOR EGG SHELLS

This trick is fun to use on Easter eggs and hardboiled eggs for the picnic basket. Dissolve 1 oz. of alum in 1/2 pt. of vinegar. With a small pointed brush, write a name or short message on the shell of raw eggs, using the alum-vinegar solution as ink. When the eggs have dried, boil the eggs gently about 12 minutes. The writing will disappear from the egg shell and will show up on the egg white when the egg is peeled.

An ounce of prevention in the garden is worth a long ton of cure. Preventive measures are easy and practical in the small kitchen garden: cleanliness, neatness and daily attention.

You will have a headstart on cleanliness if you begin and end the garden year in winter. In late February or early March you can destroy many weed seeds and insect eggs by raking up the debris of winter and burning it. In late October and early November, remove all the bean poles and tomato stakes, corn stalks and pumpkin vines.

Once the garden is ploughed or spaded in spring, destroy weed seedlings by frequent cultivation. This is best accomplished by assigning yourself two or three rows to do each morning. Fifteen minutes a day *every day* is a good deal easier than an all-day weeding session.

A neat garden is easier to keep cultivated and is aesthetically pleasing. Two wooden pegs and a string the length of your rows will guarantee straight lines of plants. Mark seedling rows with plant tags, and mark different varieties of vegetables and flowers. Use an indelible marker and place the tags so that the writing faces north. The sun will fade most markers.

Be wary of garden fads. I recently heard an expert (complete with degrees and publications) advise the application of a handful of cornmeal around the base of plants to control cutworms. His explanation was that cutworms love cornmeal but cannot digest it. They eat the cornmeal and die almost at once. At today's prices, this would be an expensive practice. Furthermore, one cannot help but wonder whether the cornmeal would not attract mice, squirrels and other rodents. My method seems to me safer, saner and cheaper. As you set out each plant, cultivate the soil carefully. Kill any cutworms or June bug larvae that you encounter. You will probably lose some plants to the cutworms. Check new plants each morning. If you have a few reserve plants, you can replace the casualties. Before removing the original plant, sift through the soil at its base. Usually the cutworm is still there. Destroy him.

INSECT REPELLENTS

A good, general non-toxic spray to keep away flea beetles and other pests:

> 1 gal. water
> juice from 3 cloves garlic
> 1 tsp. curry powder
> 1 tbsp. soap
> 1 tsp. ground cayenne

Mix ingredients together thoroughly, making sure soap is completely dissolved. Spray plants in mid-morning after the dew has evaporated.

A non-toxic dust for cabbage worms:

> 1 qt. sifted wood ashes
> 1/4 cup table salt

Mix together well and dust over cabbage plants with an old flour sifter.

A closely planted row of *castor beans* will keep out moles and provide a handsome border.

Slugs will crawl into a saucer of *beer* and expire there. A well-cultivated garden with a minimum of boards, rocks and other hiding places is not likely to be overpopulated with slugs.

Marigolds help to keep beetles away from beans and potatoes. The low bushy types such as King Tut and Fiesta are best. Sow marigold seeds indoors in mid-March or buy a flat of well-started plants, so that the marigolds are in bloom when the vegetable plants first emerge from the ground.

Codling moths can be trapped by suspending a cupful of *molasses* from the branches of fruit and nut trees.

Charles Read, a New Jersey farmer of colonial days, advised that to foil the peach borer ("the worm at ye root"), the hulls of *black walnuts* be mixed in the soil around the base of the tree. Perhaps the best piece of advice that Read left was, "Never make an ordinary or makeshift fence."

If your garden is subject to marauding wildlife, dogs—normally considered a garden menace—may become assets. I lost most of my field corn to deer and rabbits when I planted it far from the house. Now it grows in front of the house, where my dogs can roam through and around it. A flimsy barrier of stakes and string partially protects the seedlings until they are about 2 feet tall. The dogs trample some plants in spite of this but their presence and scent keep the deer and rabbits away, so the loss is negligible by comparison.

An easy way to put in poles for lima beans is to use an auger to bore the holes. The auger disturbs so little soil that pole setting can be done after the beans are well up, which makes cultivation easier for the first two weeks or so. Commercially made poles of seasoned wood with pointed ends can be pounded into the ground with a sledge hammer.

Index